PASSION FOl

A Leeds Education

PASSION FOR THE PARK
A Leeds Education

Stephen Wade

CHAPLIN BOOKS

www.chaplinbooks.co.uk

First published in 2012 by Chaplin Books
Copyright © Stephen Wade

ISBN 978-0-9571128-8-9

A CIP catalogue record for this book is available from The British Library.

Design by Michael Walsh at The Better Book Company

Cover illustration by Laura Carter *www.lauracarter.co.uk*

Printed in the UK by Ashford Colour Press

Chaplin Books
1 Eliza Place
Gosport PO12 4UN
Tel: 023 9252 9020
www.chaplinbooks.co.uk

"The most important player on the pitch is the goalie"
Albert Wade, left back for Churwell WMC FC

"If the team's a bloody good 'un, there's no need for t'goalie"
Gordon Ledd, football hack

"They carried the fight to enemy territory"
Billy Bremner on Revie's Leeds United

"Give 'em a bit of spelling..."
Teaching method of my first Head of English

Contents

Note

My Sunday team in the following pages is very loosely based on a real team, with names changed, but could be any Sunday league outfit in the country. Hopefully, you will recognise yourself here if you grace the park before Sunday lunch. The team is any team, and every team. Any seeming insults or derogatory comments in my book are meant in the spirit of traditional changing-room banter. With that in mind, I would have given anything to be a fly on the wall at Elland Road in the home-side changing room, particularly if we were losing at half time and the Scots contingent were letting loose their vocabulary of insults.

Prologue

The Passion for The Park

Maybe you drive past them on a Sunday morning on the way to the supermarket or the church: a knot of rain-soaked men, hung-over, beer-bellied and melancholy, sitting grimly outside the door of a pub, bags around them, waiting for a battered old Dormobile to take them to the park. The day could be a September Indian summer, but is more likely to be a bitingly cold November morning when all sensible folk are wrapped in several layers and keep near a fire. But that gaggle of dedicated park footballers are the backbone of the national game. You might not think so, but you are driving past poets, dreamers, visionaries.

My dreams of football began in my Leeds childhood in the Fifties. My Dad took me to see Leeds United, but before the sleek skills of Johnny Giles and the goal-grabbing wonder of John Charles, I had seen my Dad play – as right back for Churwell FC. If you don't know the village, it's between Leeds and Morley, and a mile from Elland Road. They played on the old tanhouse, an expanse of grass bordered at one end by a heap of wrecked cars and the other by a field of cows. My Dad was considered hard but fair; he parted his greased hair down the middle, as if done with a machete. He enjoyed several post-match pints, after giving everything he had, all his mental and physical resources, to that team. I was smitten with the Passion at that point. Don Revie and Billy Bremner confirmed the view that football was about winning, of course, but also that it was more about letting your body do something for a purpose, along with other men also striving for the same thing – a purpose which to onlookers must seem trivial, but in fact is wonderfully absurd.

At school I realised it was a sort of test, all this sport business, and I never bothered. But the real meaning of football was revealed to me when I first signed up to play for a works team.

The Churwell WMC team. My dad is on the back row, fourth from the right. The smiles cover the dread of heading the old laced-up bladder called a ball which was really like a sphere of granite

I played outside right for Rose Forgrove and I began to know the true depth of penance and suffering involved in the game. The idea, if I had to explain this to those unlucky people who have never played in a league, is to create an atmosphere somewhere between a battle and a playground. Everybody knows, deep down, that the yellow and red strip is ridiculous; that the shin-pads give you no protection; that there is likely to be dog-muck in the goal-mouth, and that someone is bound to call you a wanker before a ball has been kicked.

But for 90 minutes the park footballer is beyond reality – the kind of reality embodied in the foreman, the wife and the clock. He has a cause: primarily himself, and his esteem. Just the sheer satisfaction of clearing a ball and hoofing it towards the nearest roof can give that elation of the complete farewell to reality. Time stops on a Sunday in that sense and in that place. Of course, it means that the creeping sadness you feel when the ref looks at his watch with three minutes to go and you're two-nil down is the hardest thing in the world. Yet that is not the sort of time that gets you up for the six o'clock shift or the school taxi-run.

Rose Forgrove FC lacked a game-plan. They lacked the skills necessary for success, but they had the two completely indispensable qualities for park football: humour and pack-mentality.

So your centre-half is slow and his run reminds you of a rhino-charge rather than a Linford Christie sprint? So what? And the keeper tends to retch for the first ten minutes of the game, still suffering the effects of a Saturday night binge. There to be cherished is the yelling of the defence at the forwards to 'Get their fucking finger out' and the desperate screaming of the forwards at the defence to 'Clear the fucking ball!' This, together with the high comedy of the 'manager' on the touchline giving dodgy advice such as 'Chop him' or 'You're dropped, Wade!' provides the real substance.

The humour is the real pull, though. I've known players who only seem to be there on a Sunday to provide laughter, in any way they can. Typical example might be the fart in the changing room (giving rise to curry jokes and eviction of the offending party); the goal celebration (no kisses or dance, but often a punch in the ribs or a rub of mud to the nose). Most exuberant of all has to be the Teaser. This guy is merciless to anyone who shows even a hint of not being altogether ready to die for the team. Prime victim here is the Married Man. In Park Passion you have to prove that, though married, you are alive and a thorough nuisance. The Married Man must not arrive tired, or there will be marital bed jokes throughout the game. The Married Man must not be first to go home after the game, and must join in the drinking, either for misery or celebration.

The changing room has to be a slum. Preferably an old leaky hut, but other details of accommodation are useful too, such as a dripping corrugated iron roof, evidence of vermin in the floorboards and wainscot, and most of all a shower unit with patches of orange rust, leaking pipes and loose fittings.

The language is also the centre of the Park Passion. The expletives need not be varied, but they must be plentiful and directed at the defenceless. Example: the opposition striker is notably off-target and lacks speed. He is fairly entitled to be a 'Fat Bastard' for the 90 minutes. Also, the adept and successful player must learn to mime this rich Anglo Saxon, particularly when addressing the referee.

There is also the question of pitch-names. These can be affectionate, manly or abusive:

Affectionate – Wadey

Manly – Well in, good tackle, Wadey

Abusive – Stroll on, wanker.

Yet, despite these handicaps, the basic absurdity of the game co-exists, if uneasily, with its beauty and grace. Every team I've played in has had its Mr Skill and its player who once had trials with someone or other. Often, there is the star who had the awful injury when young and should have been the new George Best. Maybe the most informative case study here is the Hard Man. In later life, in the Regional League, I found myself placed in that comical category. But I realised early in my career, particularly when playing for Leeds Inland Revenue against East End Park (rumoured to have Leeds United juniors in the line-up) that you can do without the Hard Man, and that he is there as a sort of bone in the corset. We lost 10-1 and the Hard Man couldn't get within three feet of their forwards.

Dad on the Touchline

A more terrible prospect than the best opposition can be your mates – or even your family – on the touchline. My first game as a league-player was like that. My Dad and a crowd of old-timers came along. They never came a second time. I remember a high ball coming down at me from a height of seemingly a hundred feet, and my failed attempt to trap it. My Dad said, "Nice effort" but a chorus of other voices called me a wassock and hinted I was 'like a lass.' Also, dads on touchlines tend to talk about the days gone by when men were men, balls were heavy as rocks, and you could gouge an eye out with a football-lace. They love to remind you that goalies could be shouldered into the net, that a good tackler gets in first and never backs out, and that every decent player should know how to put a dislocated finger back in its proper place when the goalie's tried to stop a pile-driver.

Dads on touchlines have a bad press, and this is down to foul language, and a tendency for them to forget that this is just a game, not a place of therapy for their fractured sense of identity to be repaired by scream therapy.

Criticism is something you have to live with. There is a breed of drongo who waits for every Sunday with relish. His aim is to unsettle you and his tactics are immoral. He chooses a particular player and tries to destroy the joy in the game by creating a will to murder in the selected victim. Early in the game, his cry will be, 'Shape up number five.' Then you slip before a clearing attempt and you hear 'Clumsy bugger number five.' This is just at the point when you want to move on and forget it happened. Finally, you become the centre of the universe: 'You've two bloody left feet, player...' and 'Donkey... you're a DONKEY number five.' Often, this drongo is your opposite number. Strikers sometimes spend more time talking you down than playing the game.

So, What's This About?

I wanted to write about the ordinary lover of the beautiful game: the man in that pub car-park, with his dreams untarnished in spite of advancing years, expanding midriff and lack of a decent sprinting pace. There seem to be plenty of books about celebrating the lives of the professionals, but what about the dedicated park lads who turn out week after week, in the hope of beating another pub team or works team and creeping up Division Six of the Saturday League? The best way I can explain this 'material' is to take you to a Sunday in 1982 on a park in November, when there was a snowstorm and a bitterly cold wind. My team, North Kinley College, were playing the local Polish Club, having difficulty picking out players. I was holding my sleeves over my wrists to stave off frostbite. We were a goal up and no-one wanted to call it off. Then the game stopped and all heads turned as we saw an ambulance driving over the next pitch. We learned later, stiff as boards, that someone in the match on the pitch further up had been hospitalised with exposure.

That epitomises the joy, the celebration, the insanity and the sheer creative derangement of the Park Passion player.

So I want to tell the story of North Kinley College FC in its glory years of 1977-1984, when it went from assorted players with vaguely blue shirts and shorts to a smartly uniformed team which won the President's Shield. It will be the story of thousands of teams across the British Isles. I want to dedicate the book to Baz Fletcher, local footballer par excellence, a Renaissance man who read *The Guardian* from cover to cover every day, found time for local politics as well as a full-time teaching job, and most of all, he was the man who scored the goal of the season for 1981, slotting a drive in the top left-hand corner from 30 yards and never claimed it was just good luck.

But this is also the story of a steel town and some of its people. I came to Scunthorpe in 1974. I had married just a year before and we came across the M62 with all our worldly goods on the back of a truck. We were moving into a small terrace house in Ashby, and on our first shopping trip up the high street, we saw the windows of the Co-operative store on Broadway all smashed. I asked someone if this was a place with a violent crime problem. It looked like a tank had ram-raided the place, and ram-raiding was a new art then.

He looked at me as if I were an alien. Then he explained about the massive explosion at Flixborough power station a month before. The crack had been so powerful it had smashed these windows, about seven miles away.

Scunthorpe, which with Sheffield was a place defined by steel, was on a roll then. The Anchor Project had been initiated: a whole range of new facilities and ore preparation methods, entailing the building of Anchor Village, which was to provide temporary housing for a massive influx of labour. The whole scheme was completed the year I arrived.

This meant that at the technical college the classes were full; there were apprenticeships in the thousands, and I was to teach General Studies and English. To understand the English teacher, we need to go back to the Leeds roots and the empire of words which was built around him, offering meaning, imagination and a sense of being.

1

A Secondary Education

There I was then, going to Osmondthorpe Secondary Modern School in 1959, just as one of the world's most revolutionary decades was about to begin. There never was a more ill-equipped kid on the verge of young manhood. I was what is familiarly known in Yorkshire as a 'gawp'. In my case, this flexible insult was caused by my lack of expertise in anything practical. A gawp could not understand the wiring of a plug; he could not remember his middle name if engaged in the Battle of The Little Big Horn in his crowded head; he could not explain the function of a micrometer, let alone draw one.

As a gawp, I could not be trusted with anything such as fire or hot metal, or timing devices. I was allowed to help with wallpapering and, as time went on, I became big brother to my younger siblings and had to look after them after school because Mam had a lock-up shop at the other side of Leeds and Dad was working late in the bakery. Looking after them meant making them beans on toast for tea, then watching *The Lone Ranger* or *William Tell*.

The only object I ever recall making with any degree of success was a bow and arrow, created when I was Crazy Horse, a phase that lasted about a year. I had a wigwam and a head-dress and had learned to go walla walla, flapping my hand over my gargling mouth. I even threw an axe at the paper-boy once. He was less than tolerant and chased me up a tree. That was another element in Sioux life: my tree-house. There was a wall along the back of the garden, with a line of three trees against it, so making a rudimentary house was easy, with planks across the wall and boards of wood as walls.

All this hardly prepared me for my intended world – to be a fitter or a draughtsman. But then, school in 1960 in the heart of the workers' Leeds was not exactly Alan Bennett. Where

Bennett raises laughs about tea-table manners and eccentric relatives, I have to set against that Leeds of church and chat a darker microcosm, in which you were 'hard' or you wept most of the day.

A secondary school for boys was a place in which every step you took in each day was a manoeuvre towards a place in the hierarchy. To be hard meant that you thumped someone every day for looking at you in the wrong way. To this day I have a loose jaw that crackles and grinds, as a result of being clouted by the Flanagan twins for being in their way as they ran down the school steps.

Being hard meant that there were some boys who would not face up to you. If you were not hard, then you joined the Stamp Club or loitered in corners at play-time talking about Captain Scott or Hopalong Cassidy. If you were not hard, you played the fool so that you were too pathetic to bother with. One day I was at my desk when the boy in front combed his hair backwards and a gaggle of lice tumbled down onto my clean page of notes on The Black Hole of Calcutta. Heads turned. I was supposed to bray him. That's what you did in the hierarchy – threaten to bray someone. They would generally slink away or go red, but if you picked the wrong one – one who wanted to be above you in the hierarchy – then you were brayed. I ignored the lice and so was considered soft.

This culture is best seen in the story of Robert who, in a science lesson, caused an explosion in the lab store-room. As a result, he was caned. I can remember his scream of revenge as he ran out, bawling at the science teacher that his big brother would come and get him.

He did come – and he brought about 30 Teddy Boys with him, swinging chains, flicking blades and spitting gum out by the school gates. It was morning break, and we all stopped playing plimsoll rugger when we heard Robert's brother shout out, "Come out Jones, we're gonna smash you..." What followed was a battle across the breadth of the car-park. The staff-room emptied. First the three big men who taught games, and then the Geography master who looked like a character from Gary

Larson. After that the less sanguine characters came, armed with sticks, canes and set-squares.

The brawl lasted about ten minutes, and then the Teddy Boys ran off, swearing loudly and threatening to come back with crossbows. I believed them, because I'd been bought a crossbow when my sister had been born. Metal crossbows were available as toys in 1960. My brother and I fired them at the garage door and it split and shredded into loose flapping bits of wood after about an hour's punishment.

But the Teddy Boys never returned. Never before at Osmondthorpe had the teachers gained such a wonderful macho image. Even the weedy, yellow-faced maths teacher strutted for a day or two. My mates, of course, all wanted to be Teds so that they could have chains and look as hard as a fitter's file.

I had no idea of this at the time, but the ideologies of 1960 were seeping into me, despite the persistence of traditional curriculum materials, such as the History class. Here we were given ripping yarns and fuzzy-wuzzy foreigners. The core of the syllabus was The Empire, with Clive, Kitchener and Churchill at the heart of matters. For a whole term there was a huge map across the wall behind the teacher, showing a pink-coloured India where 'Surajah Dowlah' or 'Sir Roger Dowler' as he became, was sorted out by Lord Clive. Clive, we were assured, had no time for folk who put Britishers down a Black Hole. The teacher was particularly fond of telling us about Rorke's Drift: that was the real stuff: a handful of redcoats taking on a million Zulus! My mates and I played and re-played Rorke's Drift for months. I can recall the Welsh accents of Ken Thompson to this day. Ken Thompson (who is probably a Brigadier by now) lived, breathed and dreamed military history, uniforms and heroism. His speciality was storming a castle with the paratroopers. He would fill a castle with Germans, then douse the castle in oil, before firing a lighted match from a toy cannon at it. His mother always had a pan of water handy by the back door for when she saw the flames rise.

History was armies and hierarchies again. The British were hard. The Americans were hard. The French were suspect in this regard, being too fond of sitting about eating and sipping foul spirits; the Russians were all right if they were Cossacks, but otherwise they were too fond of singing and living in deep snow. The central pride of the syllabus was the Indian Mutiny and the way we put things straight after the atrocities. Never a mention of the Dyer massacre of course: not a word about our civilised habit of strapping men across cannon and firing the balls through them as a punishment for revolt against the Union Jack.

At times, this grand baloney world of war and derring-do wandered uneasily into actual life, like the day my friend's big brother reminisced about his military service in Aden in 1957, and talked with obvious glee about rounding up some locals, locking them in a room and setting fire to it.

My father had been hard as well, so that reinforced things. He had been in the navy against Hitler; he was a tough full-back on the football pitch, and he stood no nonsense from anyone. But he was also the typical Good Dad of the Sixties; the man who had done his bit to bring order back to the world so there was still the British pint at a shilling and twopence, the Saturday match and the week in Filey. But he also gave more than the call of duty in small, loving things such as making a medieval castle for a Christmas present, painted with home-made eggshell effects. He taught me how to ride a bike, spending most of a Saturday afternoon running down the street with one hand behind the saddle coaxing me into confidence.

He didn't understand education. He had no idea why I should like doing French. I was doing French at a secondary technical school – not much use in an apprenticeship at a Leeds engineering company where they might be making tanks or bazookas. But he knew it was important, and came along to meetings when he had to, to talk about progress or otherwise. It was usually otherwise: I had failed the 11-Plus and then the 13-Plus because numbers were as alien to me as girls' giggles.

But 1960 in Leeds for the workers was not about politics; no talk of international incidents or the Iron Curtain. No, talk ran to Leeds United and John Charles, or Bradford Northern and the Rugby League Cup. You could talk about sport, tell jokes, and most of all, tease.

Teasing was an integral part of growing up. At Osmondthorpe, all the boys had nicknames. I had several, starting with 'Monsieur' as I was good at French, then moving on to 'Cleve Tade' because I was soft; and then, after winning a few fights, I was respected again and called Paddy because I raised a few laughs with my bad Irish accent. To my relatives, I was 'sackless' – a word I later relished, as it sounded so expressive of someone lacking in sack, and you would hate to be short of that, whatever it is.

We bookish types were found out, though. The bravado and bluffing could not last long in the face of the Circuit Training Test and the Horse. Our games master was proud of his fitness suite. It was a hall full of wall-bars, with lots of thick mats and a jumping-horse. We had to scramble up and down the wall-bars, climb up ropes, go over a tall metal frame, and then sprint towards the wooden horse and leap over it, ending in an upright position and smiling broadly at him as he stared at us, ready with his teasing name for the weaklings. One poor boy, always without the proper gear and so performing in underpants and vest, would be called Wee Willy Winky as he lay down, breathless, by the horse.

And now for an interlude in my story. I've picked some heroes from the Revie days. No apologies for the nostalgia. We can't help being stuck in the era in which we first felt the worship.

Revie's Leeds Heroes 1

The Black Flash

In the team photograph in the official Leeds United handbook for the 1964-65 season, there are the established names – Charlton, Collins, Hunter and Reaney – and the rising stars at the back, including Jimmy Greenhoff. The four rows of men stand in the usual way, with arms folded, and they wear the white strip, the one they are defined with. Don Revie had adopted that to copy Real Madrid. The faces are stern, concentrated, dour. But beneath the listed names there is the line: 'Albert Johanneson was absent when the above photograph was taken.' Those words carry what was then an unwritten story. The fast left winger, terror of the best defences, was absent. Everything about that picture was white – the strip and the faces. What an irony that image has.

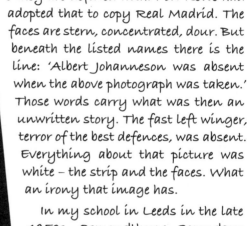

In my school in Leeds in the late 1950s, Osmondthorpe Secondary Modern, my mates and I played rugby in the playground, using a school cap for a ball. We supported Bradford Northern or, of course, Hunslet. The sports master was a Welshman who had us all playing rugger and the wide playing fields of Halton had no football nets for us. It was not a round-ball school, and Leeds was not a round-ball town. That is, until Don Revie.

My Dad used to play for Churwell WMC and he was a solid left back. The team used to play on the Tanhouse, within a mile of Elland Road ground, and it was he, Albert Wade, who took me to my first Leeds United games. One day, flushed with excitement, he said, 'Steve, there's another Albert playing today, a little winger, and he's from South Africa.' The man was Albert Johanneson, and even now, writing this, I feel the emotion well up and I have to fight it back. To anyone who is not familiar with the glorious game in the 1960s, I have to remind them that 'footballers don't cry' and that if you took some stick, you gave it back harder. Even his name stuck out, after reading the programmes with names like Wilbur Cush and Willie Bell, Grenville Hair and Freddie Goodwin. Johanneson seemed exotic, special, a word from far away. But the element of tragedy is never far from the Johanneson story, as he ended his life a forgotten man, the man not in the picture.

In 1963, when magnificent things seemed possible for Leeds, and in Elland Road, not at Headingley, the excitement was palpable and the players were celebrities. I can recall my Dad taking me to a Fairs match at which United thrashed Ferencvaros, and after, he took me to a Holbeck pub to watch Jack Charlton enjoy a meat pie and a pint. Footballers were something special then. Before that, the buzz had been when Freddie Trueman played a benefit match at Whitkirk and the whole school went to see him.

Arguably, there are two definitions of football: the attractive one is that both teams play with style, skill and speed and they are allowed to express their natural talents in speed and ball control; opposed to that is the notion of football as a conflict of kicks, flailing arms and crunching tackles. Albert Johanneson was nurtured on the stylish definition. He then found himself in a world dominated by the second one. In English football there has always been the concept of the 'gentleman' and good sportsmanship. He would have gone along with that, but not with threats to break legs and throw punches when the ref turned away.

Johanneson, the Black Flash, came into that football mentality when Revie signed him from Germiston Colliers in Johannesburg in 1961. Albert told that story in 1965, when Leeds celebrated what they called 'their triumphant year': "I was playing with a local club called Germiston Colliers back home when one day a man called Mr Gofney came along and told me that he would pay my fare to England if I would have a three-month trial with Leeds — and that he would pay my fare home again if either I did not like it or if I failed to make the grade."

He made the grade alright. He was not the first black player at Leeds — that honour goes to Gerry Francis — but when I stood in the sweeping round area of Elland Road next to the Gelderd Road end and watched him dash down that wing, I knew how special he was, and when he became known as The Black Flash I felt that to be one of the best nicknames ever.

Revie was new at Leeds and the team were languishing in the second division when the rebuilding started. The Don steadily gathered the kind of team he wanted, and at that time, wingers were absolutely crucial to success. John Charles had rejoined the team after his spell at Juventus, and I saw him play after his return. There he was — this massive V-shaped chest on thick legs steaming down the centre of the pitch, bodies seeming to bounce off him. He would expect the right kind of cross and Albert Johanneson was one of the men who would do that with accuracy, with a good strike-rate of balls just waiting to be nutted in.

Let's start with the formative fact in Johanneson's existence: apartheid. It's hard to imagine what that must have been like: to have lived in that society, with racial classifications of citizens, and black Africans considered to be the underclass, the inheritors of that word used by the old Imperialists — kaffir. Germiston, where he first played, is a gold town: today it is in the Ekurhuleni Metropolitan Municipality, and its biggest football club now is Moroka Swallows FC. It was always about gold-digging and railways, since John Jack from Germiston, Glasgow, got rich there. Over time, though, it has spawned great sports professionals, including golfers and fast bowlers.

Johanneson came from a place where he was at the end of the queue in a white world, and he had to carve a notch in the place that school had taught him was the home of Imperialistic racism. There is no surprise that he had a tough ride. But shine he did, playing once with the other black player at Leeds, Gerry Francis, and starting very positively, making his debut at Swansea, an event he wrote about: 'I think that game was the greatest thrill in my life, followed by my first home match and the semi-final at Sheffield.' He was injured in the semi-final that year, but there he was at Wembley, and we have the statistic that is always placed next to his name in the books: 'the first black player to take part in the FA Cup Final.' The semi-final had been against Manchester United, and ended with no score, then in the replay at the City Ground, Nottingham, Leeds won 1-0. In three seasons, Leeds had gone from second division obscurity to being second in the top flight, and the final was tightly balanced, Liverpool coming out 2-1 winners.

It is generally considered that his performance in that final was the beginning of Johanneson's slide from the assurance he showed when dribbling through defences, to the dark regions of uncertainty where confidence begins to fray. In the 1964 season he had been the top scorer and in one of his best games, against Newcastle, he had shown all the skills he was to be remembered for. He was that rare thing, a winger who could beat men and match the central strikers – at that time such ability was very scarce. As Rick Broadbent wrote in his book on the Leeds stars, 'That was Johanneson at his best. Dazzling, enchanting and brilliant, the swish of the svelte striker descending on goal was a sound to be feared.'

That 1965 Cup Final, according to Bobby Collins, the 'midfield general' for Revie's team, was when Johanneson 'froze'. Collins certainly knew about fear. He was one of those players who really knew how to use mental torment on the opposition: the other team were the 'enemy' to him and winning was all that counted. By his standards, Johanneson would fall short. In that final, Ian St John grabbed the winner, Leeds lost and to make matters worse, they were pipped for the championship by Manchester United, losing out on goal average. Leeds had become accustomed to success and the joy of victory: it was a huge letdown, but the town still gave the team a civic reception and I can remember my dad singing the Hilton song and the line: 'The lads at Elland Road are pals of mine...'

They were like pals. You felt you knew them, such was the curiosity about their characters, and a big brother like Albert Johanneson would have been great: gentle but fast, skills oozing out of him. At that time kids on the Gipton estate used to have football matches with anywhere between 15 to 35 players a side, and all ages could stop and have a game. There was a black lad who came to join in, and everyone, young and old, would shout, 'Albert, Albert!'

In the 61/62 season, Johanneson shone in the famous game against Chelsea at home which featured the return of John Charles. Fans around our street could talk of nothing but Johanneson after that game – the high drama of the match had included a player down with a broken leg, but Johanneson scored the goals and received a long ovation at the end. That is the Albert Johanneson we need to celebrate, defining him by the stunning power he had to shimmy past defenders; but history has fixed his identity as the man who died lonely and drunk in a Leeds tower block, on 28 September 1995. His nephew, the boxer Carl Johanneson, adds something else to that: ' It wasn't the drink that killed him –it was when his wife left him and took their two kids with her...'

The decline was sad whichever way we look at it. Johanneson was replaced by Mike O'Grady and then by Eddie Gray; his future was playing down the divisions at York City. He was 31, and at York he played a part in their promotion, but a combination of injuries, personal problems and a loss of self-assurance proved to be a lethal mixture. The obituaries and the poignant story of his death have fixed his identity in the records as the man who died of drink, his body not being discovered until days after his death. The last pictures show clearly his ill health and his weight gain.

Yet I have written this to insist that all lovers of the great game place Albert Johanneson in their minds not as the name on the gravestone at Lawnswood, a template for the failed star in his cups, but as the man who said, in 1965 when he spoke to the press: "The warm-heartedness of the people has made me love Leeds and the way the fans sometimes chant Al-bert, Al-bert, always makes me glow inside. It is nice to be part of a club and a city like Leeds, and so I thank you."

If John Charles was the Gentle Giant, then Albert Johanneson was the Giant Gentleman.

The deaths of the older generation seemed to come with alarming regularity in the early Sixties. The four grandparents who had weathered the storms of two world wars and brought up very large families seemed to be fading away. First, Granddad Schofield died in hospital; then Grandma Wade died at home, and was closely followed by her husband. My first dark sense of the inscrutability and mystery of the business of dying came when I had a glimpse of Granddad Wade in a bed placed in the corner of the sitting-room, surrounded by daughters and daughters-in-law. He was being given a cup with a special lip to drink from, and a pot was taken from under his body.

There was fuss, then there was business, and then he was put in a large brown box and taken to Cottingley cemetery where his dead son and daughter lay, just a quarter of a mile from Elland Road football ground.

"He'll hear them shout at the Gelderd Road End..." my uncle said.

But there was still Grandma Schofield, with her flowery dress and her ever-present pinny, and her large hat which had a hat-pin like a dagger rammed through it against the Yorkshire winds, which bite like cats and leave you red-faced like a Siberian. She was Florence, but Flo to most. Grandma Flo would take me out: anywhere would do – on picnics, or to watch the soldiers drill at Pontefract Barracks. She loved the pictures, and would take me to the Shaftesbury on York Road. One day, though, her fondness for feeding me boiled sweets would enter family mythology. In the middle of an exciting yarn from the days of Empire, a sweet lodged in my throat and for a while it seemed like I was heading for Cottingley as well.

She panicked, ran out to the foyer, slapping me on the back, and screaming for the manager. After a massive and shambolic set of strategies to shift the thing, it slid a bit further down and I could just suck in some air. It took about an hour to slither down to the stomach and she was in trouble from Mam that night. But you couldn't ask more of that Saturday matinée with Flo. The highlight was always the latest exploit of Don Winslow of the Navy. He was largely responsible for the pink on the map, I guess. One week he was pursued into a very spacious cave by about a hundred rabid Arabs, followers of the 'Mad Mahdi', and then, minutes later, he emerged unscathed, a look of triumph on his manly brow. The next day that Ken and I, with Ronnie Gray (whose story I shall tell shortly) twagged off school, we were Don Winslow of the Navy, Crazy Horse, and Gordon of Khartoum, all loose in Crossgates, being a nuisance to any adults trying to shop or earn a living.

Grandma Flo had had a tough life. She had brought up seven children, living in Beeston and Hunslet during the Thirties, often on the poverty line and needing the pawnbroker for survival. She was part Scottish, her mother having been seduced by one Tommy Argyle, miner and drifter. Flo had left school at 13 to earn money, and the Argyles then, in 1912, were living at a place called The Run, Middleton – a wild part of Leeds even to this day. She looked Italian, with her rich black hair and finely formed thin face. When I first saw pictures of Mary Pickford, the forces' sweetheart, I thought of Flo. As I said, she specialised in trying to see me die by choking. Another time at home she fed me gooseberries and again one of these things lodged in my throat. I was in danger of turning blue before the object went down. The Heimlich Manoeuvre was unknown in Leeds at the time. If mentioned, it would have been defined as one of Revie's football strategies. See Billy Bremner with that pass

– a Heimlich Manoeuvre if ever I saw one, our Fred! Flo would have thought it was all German and refused to learn it anyway.

Flo used to call me her Old Cock Sparrer and sing songs from the music hall; she loved Nat Jackley, the old-time star comedian who contorted his body and did silly walks long before John Cleese. I went to see him with her once. He was like a rubber man, and I tried to imitate him but was warned off because of the crick in my neck. At the Leeds Empire he stamped across the stage accompanied by cymbals and drums as he swivelled and turned, seeming to shrink his head down into his neck – maybe a useful skill for a future defender who sometimes needed to shift his neck out of the way.

Her husband, Joe Schofield, was always a mystery, a quiet man. There are two photographs of him in existence: in one he is regaled in the usual feminine drapes and flounces of baby studio photography of about 1900. In the other, he stands between two soldiers, with him wearing cotton trousers and an off-white shirt. To any normal person, it conveys the grim situation of a man under arrest. But in Schofield mythology, he is simply a cook standing between two uniformed friends.

Joe Schofield, my granddad c1917. He claimed that the guards were his mates, but he was probably under arrest for cooking bad pies

This was entirely typical of the man: silence. In the old Great War photo he looks very like Alan Ladd, with the same glower and thin blonde hair, parted severely. If he was a cook, then it was basic stuff. My brother and I tasted Granddad Schofield's cooking in 1959, when our sister was being born at home at the other side of Leeds. Joe made Army Porridge – a hard gruel with salt. Then there was his speciality breakfast, baked beans in dripping, fried until they were oozing in the stuff. If this was fed to the troops, God help them.

By 1959, Joe Schofield had had enough; he'd seen two wars and sent sons off to fight in the last one. His eldest son had come back with tales of seeing Mussolini strung up by the mob and of killing a Japanese soldier in Burma. Joe listened to everyone's stories but very rarely told any of his own. Later in my life, I began to understand this, not as being miserable or even just indulging in the famous Schofield sulk, but just that he wanted to forget, and he wanted a quiet life of sucking his pipe, having a pint at the local, and playing with grandchildren.

His trade was a bricklayer, so he had known a pattern of being laid on and off, or adapting to seasonal and casual work. He had gone down to London to help rebuild places during the Blitz, but never spoke about that either. He was solidly built, a typical Leeds grafter, but unlike the average Yorkshireman in that he had no interest in sport. He lived half a mile from Elland Road but I never recall him going or taking an interest. His generation, in fact, were destined to be the ones we look back on with an understanding nod: "Well, he's done his bit... leave him alone." They were a silent lot, who had known the worst privations, seen horror, death, poverty and disease, and carried on.

The ethos of both the Schofields and the Wades was the absolute belief in the family as the centre of the universe – the family in its furthest reaches, not simply the main pool. Everyone was expected to keep to the attitudes that had been instilled in them: you were supposed to be close in every way, both geographically and emotionally. You were rarely expected to speak, but you were always expected to act. Children were welcome at the frequent clan gatherings but to be seen and not heard. When the young lovers married, they had to visit the parental home quite often, to display their offspring, to gossip and to do things for the older generation – mainly compliment them and provide scaffolding for the egos.

The Wades of Churwell and Morley were long established in those valleys. I have trawled through pages of burial and birth lists from the Morley Old Chapel, going back to around 1760. There are a few Wades, linked with a Bradford base, up to about 1840, and then they come thick and fast in Morley: lots of early deaths, their names so typical of the time and place – George, William, John, Fred, along with the sad statements about those who never had a name at all – 'a child of Isaac Cryer'. But by 1880 there was a Harry Wade, and my guess is that he was the father of Granddad Wade – Fred Wade, who was born around 1900. As I explain elsewhere, I've also found Geordie ancestors – something my older relatives would have trouble accepting.

My dad with his mum, Nellie, around 1935. I found out just a few years ago that she was the village midwife. Looking at my dad, I reckon he was a tough delivery

Morley, Churwell and Gildersome, all settlements sprinkled around that patch of Leeds south of Holbeck and Beeston, always had their wonderful stories. In my childhood, uncles and aunts really did tell stories when you sat with them and gobbled scones and jam tarts. My favourite was the story of the Jewish cemetery in Gildersome, where my father's aunty and her bookie husband lived. The tale was that a Jewish man. settling there in the nineteenth century, suffered the death of his only daughter and wanted to bury her in a Jewish cemetery, but there was no such thing. He asked the great Lord Cavendish if he could have a small plot of land, and he was given one big enough for a shack and a grave, but then others of the Hebrew faith came and it grew. My uncle described seeing this first grave, and told me that he had said a prayer, a Christian one, but so what?

That small cemetery was later belittled by an ironworks and a main road, I guess, but I never visit the White Rose Centre or Elland Road without thinking of it. As a child, I used to walk across the stretch of land known as the Tanhouse to Gildersome to visit Aunty Francis. She and Uncle George Todkill lived in a terraced house, one row in the midst of open fields, and they had a beautiful black metal kitchen range. I loved watching her bake, sliding in a tray of buns or scones, and then seeing a huge kettle steam above the small, hot, open fire.

It was somehow a collision with a strange other world, going across to Gildersome. At the age of five or six, wandering across the farmlands owned by Mr Addiman was an adventure. First you walked past heaps of rotting old metal cars, then the football pitches, and into the fields. It was while stopping at the beck one day that I first had that childhood shock of the otherness of creatures; my cousin and I got hold of an eel, and we cut into it with a very sharp knife. The oozing flesh and the rock-hardness of the tough texture of its life was an opening into a mystery for me. It came to represent the different, sacred world out of the village and in open land where such things were found. I had nightmares for months about giant eels swallowing the house.

Later, when I studied Dialectology at the University of Leeds with Stanley Ellis (the man who studied the Yorkshire Ripper tape), I was asked to explain the etymologies of these places, but, odd as it seems now, I had never thought about it before. The reason is that, in some mysterious way, I had refused to look into meanings, because that would kill something, crush a sense of awe that I wanted to perpetuate. So when I was first told that Churwell was simply 'the well of the churls' I felt that this was to reduce a massive chunk of complex history down to a one-liner. It just wouldn't do. I can recall making Gildersome into a meaning all of my own, to counteract this. For me it meant, and still means, 'looking like shining gold' on a par with 'awesome' or 'winsome' – powerful old words that mean something dark and beautiful.

The Elland Road terraces were the ideal places to hear the dialect come alive. There was plenty of aggro and abuse, but humour with it as well. One entertainer who always stood well back offered advice to the referee and linesmen, usually along the lines of 'Gerra reet hee-ad on thee and screw in some new ees'. To his credit, he tended to say 'Tha gert gormless tatie' rather than any extreme obscenity.

The 1960s in Leeds were not all sweetness and light. I used buses and so was often around the central bus station, and recall being there waiting for a bus when there was some kind of emergency across the road by the parish church. This turned out to be a murder, and it took place where tramps used to gather and fall out, too much in drink.

Mary Judge was well known around the area of Leeds along Kirkgate, between the parish church and the Regent Hotel. It is a few streets of dark alleys, not far from the Calls – notoriously unsafe places for walks by night 40 years ago. But Mary, a cheery, sociable person, liked a drink and liked that area: in many ways a risky business, as may be seen even today, because there is a patch of land (now a small park and well maintained) under the railway arches. The trains above tend to swing around on the viaduct before going on into the station a short way further into the centre of the city.

Mary was discovered just before midnight by a passer-by on 22 February 1968, battered and mostly naked, with her clothes scattered around her body. She was only five feet five, with brown hair, and had been wearing quite garish clothes, definitely not colour-co-ordinated, so that would have made her noticeable. Her skirt was dark blue, her shoes green; she wore a white blouse, and her coat was a black check. She had severe head injuries.

The area was sealed off and arc-lights set up in that dismal, shadowy patch of land. Superintendent Hoban of Leeds CID had barriers erected and asked about her life. She was well known to the barmen of the pubs around there, such as the Brougham, the Regent and other places up Kirkgate. People said she was 'always friendly and happy, liked a drink, and loved to stop and talk to children.' The patch of land is close to Leeds central bus station, and at that time the area was notorious for its attraction to beggars and tramps. Tramps would often cadge money along the bus station platforms. By day it was busy: there was a huge Pilkington's Glass office nearby, and commuter crowds would walk from the buses, past the abattoir to Vicar Lane. By night, it has to be said, the area was well frequented too – but by prostitutes. Whether Mary was on the game is not clear, but one interesting point is that she lived in East End Park, on Glendale Street. This was a long walk for her, up towards the Shaftesbury cinema along the York Road. If she was a familiar figure down by the buses, she needed a good reason to walk more than a mile down to the pubs she liked – and alone.

It was dangerous around there, for sure. But the drifters and head cases could be entertaining, like the tramp who used to board a late-night bus. He always called out, 'She calls me Georgy Porgy' at the top of his voice. I would sit upstairs, and then hear him as he dragged his plump body upstairs, and I, along with every other passenger, prayed he would sit anywhere but by their side.

On top of that, Grandma Flo was a specialist in creating fear. When we stayed at her house in Beeston, there would come a time after tea, when we were still boisterous and full of play, when she and the other adults wanted us upstairs and silent. At that point she would say, 'Upstairs, or the Any Kid Up man will be here to get you!' We scrambled upstairs and slammed the door shut. Then dusk would fall, and I used to see the stack of coats hooked on the back of the door, and in my young mind they came alive, and were my idea of the Any Kid Up Man. Oh yes, he came at you with a big stick and yellow teeth, asking if you were still up, and if so, he would put you in his bag. The Any Kid Up Man was in my mind for years: bony fingers, bad teeth, yellow eyes and a grin of extreme menace. I had nightmares in which his long fingers would be pulling at the bedclothes to check I was still asleep.

This little lad, with that semi-rural and basic, creature-like bunch of family roots, was bound to suffer culture shock in north Leeds as he entered the Sixties and secondary modern school. After all, the village of Churwell in 1950 was a few streets, a school and a Methodist chapel. Our family home in Low Fold, the white double-cottage with the smallholding attached, was unchanged since Victorian times. The family had no indoor toilet, but shared one round the back with two other families. Next to the shed that was a toilet (no drainage, just emptied once in a while) was a midden. This was a heap of night-earth, human slurry, and vegetable matter which had been considered too useless even for the pigs. Walking out behind the cottage to the toilet on a winter's night was a test for the nerves. I thought that maybe the Any Kid Up Man might live out there, rising out of the midden like a spirit of evil.

I had spent my first years running out to scamper with the hens, throw pails of gunge at the pigs, and venture into the dark henhouse to collect eggs. I had coped with the giant sow on the loose in the yard once, being harassed by the sheepdog. I thought she was going to scoff me up, and ran in fear. I had cut rhubarb, helped make mushroom soup, been lost in the rhubarb fields, and peeped into the house of Churwell's most famous resident, the playwright and songwriter, Jack Popplewell, who wrote a big hit, *If I Should Fall in Love Again*, which won the *Morning Chronicle* Song Contest in 1940. He owned Manor Farm, off the Old Road, and he grew rhubarb, no doubt for the jam factory not far away at Beeston.

This wild, freckled rascal free in the open land and scuttling from animal to animal in between story-time at school and hospital-time due to accident-prone behaviour, now found himself wearing a green suit with short trousers, walking into secondary school without allegiances to particular gangs, innocent of the music culture seeping into consciousness ('*Running bear, loves little white girl...*') and he struggled to find a mind-hold anywhere.

And my mother – what about her bliss? Certainly not the caravan holiday. The reason was that they chose the smallest shed of a place, so that money was saved for beer and ice-cream. That meant a diet of beans on toast from the Calor gas stove, and lots of take-away fish and chips. The caravans grew smaller every year. The smallest ever was a green dome the size of a pantry called 'Rosie' and the largest was a converted railway carriage (or part of one). These were all at Primrose

Valley, next door to Butlin's holiday camp. But we didn't need redcoats: we had my dad and his brothers.

It was 1957 when the most dramatic descent on Filey by the Wade clan took place: my Uncle Arthur, a publican and coalman with four older and tougher sons, took us all to the seaside freedom on his coal wagon. We chundered across the Vale of York from the redbrick sameness of the West Riding, and eventually rattled into the empty stretch of Yorkshire leading to the sea, once calling at a rangy hotel with room in the field for a wagon and a dozen kids. It was pop and crisps and hubbub: I remember when we drove into the yard, a crowd gathered to point at us and laugh. Gaggles of bairns clambered down to earth, heading for the swings; then five adults skipped down from the cab. Aunty Miriam and Aunty Dot had been sitting on their husbands' knees for 50 miles, and the ribald jokes had turned into on-going jokes.

Aunty Dot, Miriam, my Mam and Dad, together with the two uncles, downed a glass or two of beer or barley wine, and that guaranteed an ever more raucous final leg of the adventure. Aunty Dot, after a snifter, would invariably sing her Salvation Army song:

> "There is a flag that I love best,
> of all the flags I know.
> Its colours yellow, red and blue
> It's just the flag for you...."

The other travellers must have thought we were gypsies. To me it was the romantic escape from school I had longed for ever since Christmas.

I mentioned Ronnie Gray. He was my closest friend: we tended to give each other company and comfort in a world of noise, brashness and sports fanatics. We hated all that and we withdrew into an arena of fantasy which existed somewhere between the Shaftesbury cinema and Crossgates, close to where the famous Seacroft Hospital was. What we did was tell stories, and in that was the beginning of the writer in me, but strangely, we had no football tales. We were inspired by all kinds of stuff, but I think the comics were the real inspiration. There were strips of pictures of cricketers free with *The Wizard* and I used to make up stories, turning cricketers into explorers into deepest Africa.

Ronnie looked deeply deprived and impoverished, and may have been so. I never found out. He was small and thin and his clothes always seemed ragged. His glasses were held together by what looked like plasters. But he was funny: he was the best company that a strange, inward-looking lad like me could have. Ronnie entered my imagination so deeply later, when I was a young dad, that I made up stories for my son, using Ronnie as the name of my hero. I even used Ronnie's appearance to describe my unlikely adventurer, modelled also on Don Winslow of the Navy and on intrepid cricketers who sucked on sweet cigarettes (the other commodity that went along with comics).

This city I was born into was a sprawling mass of streets, stretching across several valleys and reaching up towards the Dales and the East Riding at the top, and holding a cluster of satellite towns in the south and west, strings of mining towns, mill towns or village suburbs still clinging on to an agricultural past. Then there are your real Loiners and your folk from the frontiers. I have to be a Loiner, born in the maternity home on Woodhouse Moor in 1948, just yards away from where, back in the 1830s, the crazy Irish Chartist, Feargus O'Connor had drilled his men for his 'Physical Force' reformist actions. In more recent times it was the scene of the annual feast, a magical place of carousels, shooting-ranges and candy floss.

I learned from Keith Waterhouse's book on Leeds, *City Lights*, that not only did we attend the same secondary school (Osmondthorpe CSS) but that he almost burned down the maternity home where I was born, very nearly setting fire to a pool of oil outside the building. I may well have been inside at the time, screaming for food. But at the time of my birth, I was not actually resident in Leeds: I was taken back to Churwell, a village between Leeds and Morley, where by the age of five I would be scampering about in the long grass, eating rhubarb in the fields, feedings pigs and collecting warm eggs from the black innards of the hen-house.

My dad was working on the Co-operative Society mobile grocery wagon, settling back into civvy street after his time as a stoker on minesweepers in the war against Hitler. Mam was a machinist, out of school early and a wage-earner for her one-time desperate Beeston family who had lived close to the Ordnance factory – a target of the bombers. Mam had known the poverty of those streets around Beeston Hill and Hunslet. She has recalled the weekly pawning of big brother's one good suit, the hand-me-down clothes and the bleakest hours of the Blackout.

But in 1948, after an early scare with whooping cough when I turned blue and was well slapped back into breathing, I was placed in the care of various family members on the Wade side: Granddad and Grandma Wade, Aunty Ivy (their eldest daughter) and Uncle Albert, her quarry-gaffer husband. It was to be a time of being built up on three dinners a day, the companionship of dogs and various other animals around the fold, and hearing stories of the war.

From the start, though, I was destined to be a rackety, care-worn child with odd ailments. The first problem, after the whooping cough, croup and other terrible scourges that seem to have been everywhere, was the click in the neck. Now, not many can claim such a rare distinction as a clicking neck: something that entertained the uncles, aunts and cousins for some months. I turned my head and there was a bone-scraping, cracking sound. Granddad Wade thought I had a special malformation that might one day make me invaluable in a rugger scrum, as my neck could maybe be taken in and out in some way. Aunty Ivy said it was bad luck, because everything in life was bad luck to her and she always had a story or a myth to illustrate it. In this case it was down to being handled by a rough nurse at the crucial time when I was dragged into the light of the world. But eventually I was taken to the doctor. Apparently, such clicks disappeared in the course of time and meanwhile, I had a party-trick. At birthday celebrations and at Christmas, various cousins and aunties and uncles were given a demonstration of 'The Click'. I would be placed in an upright position, head looking straight ahead, and then, with a deft but gentle shift to a sideways glance, there would be this cracking noise: nothing too horrible, but enough to make relatives wince and screw up their faces. My Grandma Wade would always say, "Ahhh. It's enough to make my bum shiver!"

But the bizarre medical case-history went on. I was circumcised. I guess that was because it was considered a healthy thing to do at the time; the world was obsessed with the future emergence of germs harboured in the sweaty foreskin. That's the tale, anyway. It's possible we were Jewish. My best friend at school, when he learned of this (and every other lad still had a full roll of flesh down there) insisted that the maternal name, Schofield, was really something Jewish like Schonfeld, and that I ought to be going to a synagogue. My ignorance knew no bounds then: I thought that was a place when your sins were rubbed out (or punished).

It grew worse: I began to have real difficulty in the final phase of the digestive process. Not to put too fine a point on it, I was most irregular in an age when regularity in the bowel-movements was considered to be more crucial to Britain than the outcome of the Korean War. More alarming yet was the colour of my stool. It was light grey.

"I can't grasp this ... it's bloody dogs what have grey shit!" Uncle Albert said.

Desperate remedies were tried. After all, this horror was happening to a lad who had the full dose of cod-liver oil every day, and the concentrated orange-juice AND the full quota of fresh vegetables. The outcome was a long session, sitting in the shared outside toilets behind Granddad's farmhouse, having soap rubbed around my rectum by Uncle Albert, a man with his own secular version of Muscular Christianity. It involved a basin of water and Pear's soap. I could never look at that Millais painting of Bubbles ever again without a throbbing sensation in my innards.

Some today might call that child abuse. In the Fifties it was homely medicine, just like the poultices. I had most varieties of poultice, some even involving mushrooms. Some amateur medico in the Wades was keen to experiment with these squares of linen packed with anything hot and strapped around the chest until you hopped around, being told that 'big boys don't cry.'

By the age of five, I had had every ailment except the Pudsey Palsy and had been warned against King Cough every time I sat bare-arsed on a flagstone. This was the time, I have since learned, when a whole generation had suffered the ravages of diphtheria and TB, and there was a feeling of revenge in the air against all unannounced bugs arriving in the village.

Otherwise, the joys of life around 1952 in the West Riding were mostly about beasts. I loved them – dogs, cats, rabbits, cows, pigs, donkeys, hens – even the occasional ferret. But my Granddad's dog, Timmy, was my best pal. I used to sit and eat rabbit stew and mushrooms in the one main room of the cottage in Low Fold and Timmy would slobber about on the floor by my side. One day I was in a faddy mood and wouldn't eat my dinner. Granddad lowered my plate and said Timmy could have it. He did. I yelled and screamed all night.

I was accident-prone as well as weirdly ill in my Churwell years. The young marrieds, Albert and Joyce, lived with me in their half of the cottage. Heating was all about coal fires, of course, and the room was hazardous. In my five years there, I put my hand in the coal fire to grab a pencil; I stuck a darning-needle in my knee; I placed my fingers under the treddle of the Singer sewing-machine, and I fell over the door-rod, splitting my head open. Uncle George took me to Leeds Infirmary in his huge black car.

It was an age of advice from the elders. All the uncles and grandparents relished delivering scraps of the wisdom they had gleaned in their lifetimes. Uncle Albert's favourite was,

'The bigger they are, the harder they fall … so hit 'em first kid!' Granddad Wade was also concerned to help in cases of bullying, and he used to show me what to do as a threat. He would hold out both fists and say, "Which one do you want … this one's Leeds Infirmary, and this one's Sudden Death!" In our pathetic little voices, my cousins and I would answer, "Leeds Infirmary please…." And then kick him on the shin and run off into the rhubarb field.

The centre of life at this time was Uncle Albert. He was a man with half a stomach but the loudest farts in Yorkshire. That was a paradox I have never been able to resolve. But he was a man of many parts. He was a quarry gaffer in Morley, and so was accustomed to getting his own way; he had a creative instinct which led him to whittle away at marquetry, and he was obsessed with betting and horse-racing. But there was a dark side. He once left out a plate of poisoned meat for the puppy next door, as the poor thing was barking at night. What he got up to in his shed was anyone's guess. But he was a man with extreme views. On reflection, I feel his real future, thankfully never fulfilled was being Hitler's disciple in the not-quite Aryan dales of Tykeshire.

He had his useful side. On certain summer evenings, he would exercise another of his myriad skills: barbering. My cousins and I would take turns at leaping up onto a high chair in the middle of the garden, and he would place a basin over our heads and create the classic short back and sides. We would all annoy him with that famous phrase from the comedian Ken Platt, whose radio programme we all loved, "Dad … Dad … If he cuts your ear off, can I have it!"

Granddad was an enigma. He worked in a tan-house, and there was a smell coming from the Mill Shaw tannery that is like no other: it comes at your lungs like a slice of acid, a blade that is going to scythe away anything that might be vulnerable. And it filled the air for hundreds of yards around the place, extending to the post-war pre-fabs built hastily by the side of Cottingley cemetery, and even to the Churwell cricket ground, where father and uncles would put on their whites and fill up a long July Sunday with their antics on and off the field.

But Granddad Wade, with his flat cap, shabby dark blue suit and fob-watch, was a man of varied abilities of survival. He had fathered 11 children, nine of whom survived infancy; he somehow always had cash for beer at Churwell Club, and above all, he had charm. True Yorkshire charm is a combination of tomfoolery and charades. I always thought that it belonged in Lehar's operettas because it takes place in a country of the Tyke's invention like the Land of Smiles: somewhere in which the whimsicality of childhood can meet the dramatic imitations of Clark Gable or Humphrey Bogart. Of course, it is difficult to be taken seriously when wearing a tweed cap and smelling of strong shag pipe tobacco.

Granddad had the ability to talk about other things besides football. He could charm younger women as well as children. My mother used to love his visits when we had moved away to North Leeds and he would sometimes come to take me fishing or to watch the beasts being sold in Wetherby or Harrogate. When he came one day, in a warm summer holiday, he whisked Mam and me away to the fields near Temple Newsam House and we had the nets on the end of bamboo canes you could buy at the corner shop, keen to land a few tiddlers. Of course, he would have you believe that pike were lurking in there, and he would become the pike, his face and hands transformed into aspects of the canny hunter's stance as he watches his prey. You could imagine the chubby little perch loitering about, unaware that a big belly and a jaw full of sharp nail-like teeth were waiting for him.

We lay back in the grass that day, jam-jars alive with tiddlers. He hummed a tune, propped his cap over his face. My Mam nibbled at a sandwich, and I asked where the pike went for their holidays... I mean, did they leave the little pond?

"Oh yes... they go to Filey like the rest of us, to see their cousins the sharks..."

"What's a shark, Granddad?"

"Well it's sort of like a very big pike."

"Oh, and is it friends with the Temple Newsam pikes then?"

"Of course... they go to Wetherby races together."

By 1955, we moved to north Leeds. I now had a brother, born in 1953 in Morley. We were scamps in nappies and later cowboy outfits, scuttering among the old lanes and farmlands around the village, but the change in our lives was going to be huge: all the way across the city to a place of crowded streets and very big schools – nothing like the village school in Churwell where we slept the afternoons away while the teachers relaxed, reading their romances or doing crosswords. No, we were to go to 'big boys' school' and the move was going to be exciting – all of us going in Uncle Harry's removal van. For every journey in the Fifties, whether for sport or work, there seemed to be the right kind of vehicle. Later on, I imagined the Wade funerals being done with the co-operation of some uncle's rag-and-bone cart or milk-truck.

So it was goodbye to Aunty Ivy's Jim Reeves records and Uncle Albert's round robins and yankee bets; no more Sunday School at the Back Green Methodist chapel, and no more jaunts across the farmland – well, not really, as we were to visit Churwell again several times in every year. But it seemed like a radical farewell, a great adventure.

Uncle Harry's huge and ancient removal van (smelling of animals, as he kept pigs) took us to a place called Halton, north Leeds, on the road towards Selby and York. For me, it was the beginning of school life proper, and a culture shock.

2

Gentlemen and Amateurs

Some History

My male relatives were not exactly articulate about football. I would go to watch Revie's team at Elland Road with Dad, uncles and friends, all in their long overcoats, and it would seem a grey, dour experience until the kick-off. The entire ritual build-up to the match would be shrouded in that particular sadness that comes from a sense of doing penance. The walk, from Beeston down the slope into Holbeck, was silent. Then the queue and the negative remarks. The crush and the fear seemed to be part of a boy's education in this Yorkshire brand of suffering.

At a cup match once, Leeds against Everton, I was genuinely terrified, and was lost in a sea of smelly solid male figures loaded down with the gloom of negative thought. But I struggled through to find the other older male Wades after a while – still in the same place. The usual wit said one of his favourite lines: "The pitch is lookin' good. I think they buried a few..." and the men felt obliged to laugh.

So where was the seed planted? The seed that would only germinate when I had left school and was drawn to football on the park as some kind of test? It came from what happened after kick-off. Slowly, inevitably, these quiet men would become articulate. They gasped at the sheer lyrical grace of Giles or Clarke, and at the powerful, manly clearing header of Paul Madeley. I came to realise that this was the expression of their souls. Those glum tradesmen, without words to express their sensitivity in the routine week, found a kind of poetry and a certain praise in their words on the terraces. This is all before obscenity too. I recall a game when we were in the Scratching Shed at Elland Road and a man a few rows back swore too loudly. Several older men turned to face him, pointing out that a young man there had his girlfriend with him, and could the language be turned down? It was, with apologies.

In fact, the men would seem to enjoy finding the right words for particular qualities. You would hear the vocabulary of respect and maleness: plucky, tough, canny, quick as a lop (a fly) and great turn, lad! Highest praise of all seemed to be 'Good effort son!' when a shot was clever and just missed the net, or when a tackle was brave but ineffective.

In this way, I absorbed a credo: a gentlemanly philosophy that gave respect to the opposition and knew what fairness was. I knew only with hindsight that the Saturday ritual, from the walk to the ground to coming home in time for the reading of the classified results, was a confirmation that there was a Yorkshire soul under the dullness and the reluctance to talk about feelings. After all, in my clan, men turned away to weep in private at funerals. There was none of this bold Irish 'Sorry for your trouble, mate.' Nobody read poems either, although they liked the Methodist hymns.

When I turned out for the Sunday teams, then, I had a vague feeling that I was a part of this genuine substance of life, the certainty that the actual touch of the turf, the green line of grass colour on your shorts and the mud in the face, was an integral part of the performance. I had absorbed the need to prove something, to be tested in some way. I had no understanding of the game, though. At school I had been one of the banished non-sporters, sent indoors to read or made to shiver in a dirty vest and pants while the real men played rugger or did circuit training. But at school it meant nothing because there was no call to be in a real community and to need to express your body and its strength and skill with style. You could be respected as a clogger, or stuck between the goalposts because you were the tallest lad in the class, but few had their heart in the games.

That First Game

But the first taste of Sunday football, the first game that became responsible for the addiction later, was as eventful as destiny could make it. It had heroism and tragedy, and as much irony as Shakespeare at his best. Rose Forgrove were to play a village team somewhere north of Leeds. The day was raw; I bring to mind the sheer cold terror of the stinking changing rooms as I put on socks caked in mud, unwashed from the previous week, and then put on shorts that were too tight for me. The boots were the cheapest available, bought in Woolworth's. They were the primitive variety that old-timers will remember, with orange piping on and screw-in studs of hard plastic that never fitted properly. The shirt was stiff as a board. I walked out like an ageing old boiler with pile problems. There was a crowd of six and two dogs.

The trainer-manager, a man of about 60 with dreams of being Bill Shankly, had oranges in a brown paper bag, a bucket of water and a packet of Elastoplasts for his First-Aid back-up. He wore a flat cap and had a scarf tight around his neck that was fixed there all week, according to rumour. His only tactical advice was "Get the bloody thing upfield."

I was young and quite fast, so I was on right wing. But I had no skill or close control. All I could do was run with the ball. The result was that I was solidly tackled by an old clogger. My first run down the wing was nippy and impressive, but I never looked up. I know that I stared at the grass beneath me, and then suddenly was felled as I met what seemed like an oak log across my path, and I fell breathless.

But our goalie was magnificent, and kept the score down to 3-1. I didn't receive any good comments at all and I found, when I took my boots off, that both toenails on my big toes had come off completely. I spent a few months visiting a chiropodist. I also had bruises everywhere and walked stiffly all week. Our centre-half had a shiner and the captain moaned and whined about how slow we were from morn to dusk every working day before the next game. 'You don't shout! No bugger shouts! I mean, you're too polite. It's like a bloody vicarage tea-party...

please pass the ball would you, old bean...'

But all this initiation in the formative years was settling in, so that when North Kinley were born, I was older and wiser, and had graduated from winger to sweeper. What I had learned by osmosis was how important it was to be a gentleman player, and to respect both the opposition and the rules. Now this introduces the delicate subject of knowledge of the game. This is one of the besetting sins of park football, and certain types of ignorance perhaps define the amateur player most accurately. These are the main bones of contention here:

The throw-in:

The Sunday footballer has only a vague notion of how far back the hands should go, and where the legs should be – fast together? One foot behind for a push? The likely outcome of this is a furtive and quick throw when the referee turns away for a second.

Off side:

Basically, the concept is popular but useless at this level. Some hopeless, winded defender on the turf, a wound across his face, fails to tackle the striker who has sprung the offside trap, and all team mates turn to give him the black look. This comes of trying to play the attacker offside when the mental agility and team communication is woefully inadequate.

Free kick:

Ten yards back is an idea that tests the basic arithmetic and geography of the teams. The referee usually paces the distance but the line moves in step with him and various players commit assaults in the ruck. The ball is inevitably booted over the stand because the striker tries a Brazilian banana kick.

Penalty:

Naturally, for one side this happens when a defender coughs aggressively towards a striker; while for the other team, felling a nippy winger who has cut in about to score is a brilliant tackle.

Ungentlemanly conduct:

In Yorkshire and most Northern areas, this is best defined as a punch to the nose or chin. In some marginal cases, it is kicking the ball away or shoving the referee into a muddy patch in the goal area.

Obstruction:

This is any offence which includes standing in front of a man to fell him with a shoulder or pulling his arm backwards. But often, totally brilliant tackles are claimed to be obstructive if a team is 3-0 down.

What really characterises the amateur game then? I soon learned that the changing room or saloon bar complaints defined this. Most popular features of the game can be illustrated by taking the reader through a typical match. Imagine the scene: ten o'clock on a Sunday morning and the teams have arrived – most of them – as a few notorious characters are late or being talked out of bed by the keenest few who take the game seriously. The pitch is ready but close observation reveals that the nets are ripped and not tightly fixed at the post, so balls could enter the net through the sides. There is no linesman, so the injured reserve is begging a bystander to run the line.

As the match begins, it soon becomes clear that the referee will turn a blind eye to virtually every foul, so the game deteriorates into a rough-house and then someone is sent off for 'cheek'. The winning goal is handed in Maradona-style and the referee didn't see it, so the prima donnas in the losing team sulk and one of them walks off, swearing loudly.

This could go on interminably. In other words, what you are up against in park football is a lack of care, knowledge and organisation. The kit is never washed and there is no spare ball. Play is allowed on unplayable pitches; studs are not inspected; substitutes could be anyone from Fred Brown to Stan Collymore. But the mystery is that there is usually a sort of higher echelon of 'management'. There is often a game plan, hatched in the Star and Anchor and discussed at great length and with increasing volume.

Amateurism also involves stunning displays of courage and self-belief against all the odds. The type of park player who symbolises the true grit and spirit of the game is the steady workman: he is carrying a paunch but sees himself as his boyhood hero; he shouts a lot so that it seems he is giving it 100 percent while all around him are slackers; he usually has one skill which is his trademark and he does it repeatedly. In one case this might be a neat shimmy or maybe a pass with a nice bend on it. But this one move he does with laboured style and it creates his nickname and his identity.

The gentleman amateur needs leadership. There is usually a power struggle between the one who has played at 'a good level' some years ago and now sees himself as the General, and the Upstart Mr Fitness. The latter reads the soccer magazines avidly and talks in a semi-intellectual way about vague concepts such as playing zones. I have listened to hundreds of conversations like this on a Sunday in the bar:

General: "See, Tommy is not, well, without giving offence, getting his finger out of his wotsit is he? We need to back him up, with Paul being available for the set-pieces and to nail that tosser who kicks everything what moves..."

Upstart: "Right, yes, but if we played zones we can save energy. You don't run about like a blue-arsed fly with this method see? The Italians are masters of it."

General: "Zones?"

Upstart: "Zones... don't tell me you never heard of zones? Hey everybody, Jim's never heard of zones!"

General: "I bloody have. It's when you play man-marking..."

(laughter and ridicule)

What nobody would admit, in company, is that they all played Subbuteo on a Sunday after the boozing session at the pub, and pretended to apply the tactics of some Brazilian coach – or even Alf Ramsey.

Enter North Kinley

It's time to focus on the team at the centre of this chronicle. The story here is one of the rise to glory of a team of lecturers and associated friends who went from unfit and ill-equipped riff-raff to honourable winners of a local cup competition. Along the way, their story is the story of your team and every team with a commitment to the park variety of the noble game.

Picture the first team and its friendlies. We had a sequence of games arranged against anyone who would take us on, and we struggled to raise a team of eleven men most weeks. But this is the roll of honour:

John was the quickest striker, thin and fit, with a loping stride and a movement like a gazelle. The only problem was he was violently sick before every game and he never walked on the pitch until ten minutes of desperate shouting had occurred. The shouting was mostly exhorting John to get his effin' backside on the pitch.

Alan was the midfield dynamo and the brains of the team. His voice was always the loudest and he was quick with a compliment or a cheering shriek. In one game, when we were 5-0 down, a high ball came down at me and he reminded me that I had to head it big and bold. "It's important, Steve...It's important." I cleared it. We still lost 5-0.

Nico was the Italian amongst us, with the Causio looks: short but strong, and very fast, with good all-round skill. He had a quick change of pace and a devastating drive. This is the player you felt gave that glint of glamour and status to the outfit, even when the team photo shows a bedraggled crew outside a rotten shack which served for a changing room when the empties and old planks had been cleared out.

Pete was the worrier. He was a defender with a sense of imminent disaster and tended to anticipate every potential leak in the defence. Pete could talk tactics until the cows came home, and had the imagination to compare the team's nature and ability to Chelsea or Liverpool. The game for him existed in some plane of vision in which every man is capable of being a Brazilian international and should be reminded of his shortcomings regularly.

Ken was the sprinter, graceful, fast and impressive with the ball. Though often he would still be running and had lost the ball 30 seconds previously. But his goals were spectacular and his sulks worthy of maybe not Hollywood but Elstree in terms of dramatic power.

Mike, the keeper, was Mr Cool. But there had been others until he was discovered. We had experienced the goalie in the 'Piggy' Lawrence mould (of Liverpool fame), the 'Fist everything and hope' type and the showy, stylish but mentally wandering keeper who was likely to be chatting to a young lady as the ball sailed into the net.

Steve (me), the sweeper: majestic in running around to no purpose, still imbued with the idea that you chase everything and forget about marking and position. His idol was Jack Charlton, but Steve was never tall enough to be a centre-half, so he assumed the role of stopper/sweeper instead. This meant regular bruises. One sore foot lasted two months, but it had saved a certain goal, so what?

Clive – really a rugby player, so hard as a shed plank. Clive inspired the defence with his sheer commitment to the tackle. Strikers feared his gallop towards them and usually passed the ball in a panic.

Phil was tall and sturdy but was a dreamer who basically couldn't shift his worries out of his mind before the game. He also tended to play backwards – that is, keeping possession with intricate runs, but going towards our goal. His philosophical frame of mind excluded him from pub debate.

Dennis was the black sheep – always in trouble, and likely to be sent for an early bath. But his true grit turned many a game and his heading ability was formidable. His towering figure was the backbone of the team. He was the quiet, reflective type, with no real interest in dissecting the game afterwards.

Baz, the natural captain, is last. He was the intellectual and Marxist who figured prominently as utility man and would play anywhere at short notice. His desire to win overcame any tendency towards self-doubt that might creep in. In fact, self-doubt could never quite be eroded in the history of North Kinley.

What about the pitches? At Bottesford we played on a pronounced slope. Somewhere near Barton we played on a bog. Goals were sometimes bent and disfigured. We played on ice and in snow; at times the game was played in the middle of a huge leisure ground with teams on all sides and you were likely to kick the wrong ball, or to stray into another game when concentration lapsed. There was even one pitch that had a cricket roller in one corner and no-one could shift it, so we played around it. We had read stories about certain professional managers supposedly watering the goalmouth to suit their own team, but that was nothing compared to the mysterious appearance of cow pats in the second half, after you had gone into the break a goal up.

But our beginnings were humble. In the pre-league days we struggled for kit and our appearance was dodgy. On one team photograph, the shivering keeper is wearing a jersey left over from his folk-club days; four players wear stripes and the others wear blue tee-shirts. Not everyone had boots. One winger played in plimsolls for a few games. We had no support staff so laundry was usually in the care of the married men. Bachelors, when they did foolishly offer to wash kit, were wont to forget and the kitbag was as malodorous as a tramp's underpants.

We did, however, show a remarkable ability to adapt and survive. One early keeper had insisted on playing in huge Chelsea boots, and this, together with his ample gut, kept a few shots out. We became specialists in goal-line clearances and falls made fortuitously so that they looked like calculated blocks. What we lost in skill we made up for in bulk, and our four defenders could more or less eclipse the goal from certain angles.

But the friendlies gradually became unfriendly and we wanted to win. The reason why was hard to fathom. It didn't matter, as there were no points to be won. But my own opinion was that it was the soul again. That basic suffering was cleansing the rotten work out of us every week, and winning was simply the crowning glory of that uplifting feeling of bone on bone and elbow on face. The limps and black eyes became somehow more worthwhile if they were to win points rather than simply comradely pats on the back.

The turning point came with a victory against quite a good team. This was the Parks Department, and we had beaten them 3-2. We played with some resemblance to a team and actually passed the ball at times – as opposed to hoping that hasty bootings would lead to something creative. Also, I remember that there was a crowd of about 20 locals and that at half time, an old man came up to me and said, "Are you the Wade from Messingham – Harry's lad?"

"No, I'm the Wade from Leeds, Albert's lad."

"Oh shame. Harry's lad were a useful player."

I didn't enjoy feeling totally mediocre – and it made me determined to improve. I even went for a jog, I recall. But the main thing was we had won and we had beaten a team who were in a league of some kind. Oh dear, dreams of grandeur stirred and the Sunday lunch talk was of nothing but that fearful phrase, THE LEAGUE. Mutterings of the word 'Competitive' were heard and it was almost put to the ballot. But in the end, it was carried, and we vowed, in our cups, to 'get fit' and 'take it seriously.' This has been the mistake of countless teams over the history of the game. It leads naturally to friends falling out and splits searing through the seamless garment of friendship. People had to be dropped when you played in a league. If you missed a tackle and the other lot scored, you could be vilified in the pub and maybe lose your place.

The change was upon us, and the innocent days of being gentlemen were wearing thin.

3

Sunday Mornings in the Tackle

This was going on in the mid-Seventies, and I was teaching in a college of further education. The local industry was steel. The place was steel town, for then it was booming. I taught everything from 'O' level English to General Studies for plumbers, engineers, caterers and secretaries. I was recently married, and it was my first job. We had moved from Yorkshire to somewhere that was more markedly 'provincial' in the sense that there was no city (the nearest was Lincoln, 26 miles away and that was too quaint and tourist-ridden to qualify). There were endless acres of green and the sky in North Lincolnshire, compared to that above Halifax, was noticeable and huge. People had large gardens and moved and spoke like country people.

As I came into Scunthorpe for the first time, I saw that it boasted it was 'An Industrial Town' and it's still true today. You arrive by car or by train and you see greenery. The parks, golf courses and wide spaces you see in the west give you no sign of any blast furnaces. The other side of town then had massive sites at Normanby Park, Appleby Frodingham, and secondary industries, all dominated by the impressive furnaces called the Three Queens.

The place had mushroomed in the late nineteenth century and labour had been imported from everywhere. There was a Welsh community; there were Scots, Liverpudlians, Irish, Geordies, Ukrainians, Italians, Poles, Spanish and Asians. It had the character of an American frontier town, and I taught them all. My first week at work included classes of child-care students and hairdressers, but mostly I taught big-boned, earthy apprentices. I was untrained; all I had was my academic qualifications and the courage (or foolishness) to stand up in front of these people and talk about semi-colons or William Shakespeare.

All this is crucial in understanding my football career, because it was linked with my need to prove my working-class heritage. I was to become the 'Doc.' At centre half, I was obviously good in the air, but I was known to be a studious type with a fondness for poetry and literary discussion, and this labelled me as weird in the eyes of some. But I had been well trained as a header of the ball. That was my great strength, and I had been coached in jumping, timing and different ways to head: I became adept at flicks, cushioned headers and glancing headers from balls coming at you with pace.

The Doc's training when young was totally manic. My father, realising in my Leeds days that I was hopeless and needed skill, started a 'Wall Game' in our back yard. Behind my mother's clothing shop there was a yard with high walls, enclosed like a squash court. Dad would play head tennis with me for hours, chalking out boxes on the walls which we had to head into. These would become duels, and as he was now unfit and long past his playing days, I did well when the skill began to sink in. This whipped him up to complete animal desire to win. Stripped to the waist, he would cover the yard with sweat and be so red that my Mam would stop the game and tell him off. Looking back, I feel sure he was bordering on a seizure, so frenzied was he in the back yard.

So now there I was, the Doc, with this strange desire to defend. Alan said to me one day, when we were holding a 1-0 lead, "You like to defend don't you?" and I realised that I did. They shall not pass was my credo. They often did, but not easily. I had a thrill when I anticipated a pass and tapped the ball back to the keeper, breaking up an attack, or when I cleared a ball after the other defenders had been caught upfield after a corner.

At college, the macho pride of my Leeds working-class family held me together, even with the toughest classes. At that time, the steelworks virtually controlled the college, as it supplied their livelihood, and over the ten years of North Kinley's league period, my playing and travelling around the county coincided with massive changes in the industry around us. But in those years around 1976-80 I had to prove all kinds of things. I kept telling myself that I could teach anything, that sheer effrontery would do the trick. There was one class of iron and steel operatives who were like animals let loose from some cage. About 30 of them swarmed over the classroom, slithering on desks, singing to themselves and having to be forced to improve their spelling with me. They hated it.

But I persevered. I took the register on the first week. That took 20 minutes, as they kept changing position and so many of them looked alike. One young man gave his name as Gavro Manisckek. He was noisy and tried to tell jokes all lesson. I shouted a lot. We finally had ten minutes of quiet time from the hour-long lesson. The week after I noticed Gavro was absent.

"Where's Manisckek?" I asked the class.

"Who?"

"The lad with the fuzzy hair and the loud voice, you know..."

"Oh, Tony! That's Tony Williams. He died last Sunday. Killed on his bike, thick prat."

Looking back, I can see that the tension got to me, and that Sunday on the park was a release, and an outlet for aggression. Yet amazingly, I was never booked. I perfected the art of nobbling and annoying the fast-forwards without being noticed, and of course, I was a gentleman. Dad had seen to that.

Revie's Leeds Heroes 2

Revie's Back-Room Team

To virtually every Leeds loiner the name of Don Revie does not need an explanation, but for the sake of the record, let's just say that he was the football manager who made the Leeds team everyone with an interest in football knows about: the one with Billy Bremner, Jack Charlton, Allan Clarke and a host of others. That team made Elland Road rock – in many sense of the word. They won a stack of major honours on the field and ventured into European competition, where they impressed. My own memories of those heady days are most vividly represented by watching a 5-1 victory over Ferencvaros, and I recall watching Jack Charlton eat a pork pie with his pint in a Holbeck pub after that.

But what about the team in the limelight – the one that kept the men going, patched them up, gave them massages, took X-rays and so on? There was Les Cocker who was a trainer-coach and coached the England team as well at one point; there was Bob English the physiotherapist and Syd Owen the chief coach. In addition to that crew, there were the staff at St James's who did the radiography.

The produced a special supplement at the height of the team's success, and journalist Terry Lofthouse asked what the secret was. It was, he was certain, in the system of which Syd Owen and Revie were the centre. When Lofthouse wrote, Leeds were contending for the top spot of the First Division, after being Second Division champions. The basis of the system was that someone would be out watching the team Leeds United were to play the following week: out there every Saturday looking closely at the next opposition.

Syd Owen had the main part of that chore, and he wrote up a long report: he told Lofthouse it was 'Sometimes 1,600 words, on a complete analysis of each of the 22 players he had seen that day.' Owen explained that the opposition players were profiled in minute detail, as the journalist summarised: 'Their strong points, their weaknesses, are all thoroughly outlined. Whether the player is a striking forward, a ball player or defender is all contained in the report. This is then filed away in the Elland Road archives for future reference.' It all seems so simple now – common practice for clubs in fact.

Harry Reynolds, the chairman at the time, explained that the result of the hard work was that Leeds had a 'wonderful spirit' and that was evident 'from the board down...'

As the team trained, there was Maurice Lindley, the chief scout, looking at potential Leeds players around the land, and Bob English who looked after the muscles and bones after each crushingly physical confrontation. The 1960s style of play was very hard and demanded toughness in close physical contact.

When Leeds United were proclaimed champions in April 1969, what Don Revie told the explains a great deal about his attitudes and why so much was achieved. After the goalless draw at Liverpool that clinched the title, he said, 'I thought our defence was wonderful. We allowed Liverpool only two chances when they looked like scoring and that's some going. We would have liked to have attacked a bit more...' In other words, he enjoyed the moment, but was still critical and thinking of improvements. A leader like that needed a back-up team of incredible devotion to the cause.

Maurice Lindley was profiled in a special commemorative brochure and it was noted there that 'he gained his wide experience with Everton.' He directed the club's scouting activities and it was said that 'he personally scours the British Isles for likely lads and has even been known on occasion to spend an evening at home.' What was written about Lindley could apply to any of the support staff: 'He absorbs work like a sponge.'

Syd Owen was captain of the Luton Town team that played at Wembley in 1960 and he was footballer of the year that season; he was widely respected everywhere and everyone knew that he was talented when it came to passing on the experience he had gathered. When Syd was asked to say a little more about how he spent his time at Elland Road, he said: 'Our job is to take the lads who join the club and prepare them for the first team selection at the earliest possible moment. The lads must be prepared to dedicate themselves entirely to the game.' He also made the point that the Leeds stars were still 'working' for the club when they were off the field.

Les Cocker was training the England Under 23 team when, in 1967, he received a tribute from the club's press-writers.

They said what was valued was his quick and accurate assessment of injuries and 'the speedy application of the necessary remedial treatment.' But more than that, he had presence, respect and a first-class career record. Bob English, the physio, was known at the time for the way he devised a series of 'graduated training and development exercises.' And there was also Cyril Partridge, a man who looked after the junior team.

When it came to medicine applied to the team and their injuries over a recovery period, pictures of the rehabilitation room as it was in the mid-60s make it look very simple and plain through today's eyes. One photograph shows Bob English in the room, treating 'Sniffer' Clarke's foot. The only technical gear present appear to be large lights and traction equipment. There had to be several pounds of liniment around too.

The official leaflet explains that 'all players are examined on joining the club and are then subject to a complete medical check each season.' But what about the hands-on hospital work, when injured players were taken across the city to receive treatment? Who was waiting for them there? One person who was there and recalls the players arriving is Liz Horsley.

Liz was working at a private radiology practice in Clarendon Road where the clients were those who either chose to pay for their X-rays or were sent by their firms, insurance companies or employers for private examinations. She has vivid memories of the sports teams who came.

"We had a constant stream of footballers – especially on Monday mornings following the weekend matches," she said. "Names that particularly spring to mind are Jack Charlton, Allan C.larke, Billy Bremner, Peter Lorimer, Norman Hunter and Gary Sprake. I remember also young and up-and-coming players at the time – such as Terry Yorath."

Liz has a clear recall of a time when Jack Charlton came after an important Wembley game and she discovered that he had been playing the match with a broken toe. Football fans always suspected that Big Jack was made of iron. Then there was the occasion when Billy Bremner brought his son – that was nothing to do with football, but the boy thought he could fly like Batman and had done so from a bedroom window. Luckily, the damage done was limited to a broken arm.

Leeds United fans have always had a bad press and many football people are always keen to bring to mind embarrassing occasions, such as the time Leeds fans destroyed rows of seating at Derby's ground; of course there have been legendary rough-house rucks, but at the base of all this, from the 'scratching shed' to the Gelderd Road end, the massed Leeds fans have, in my experience, the two most essential attributes of real football folk: philosophical acceptance and endless optimism. In the early Revie era my strongest memories from the match and the terraces are of being surrounded by big, overcoated men who guffawed and swore, but who also went hoarse telling a player he was doing alright. There was a sense, even to a kid, that something exciting was happening, and the applause was heartening. We still had the terrace comedians, like the man (always at the back) who made bizarre comments about the linesman's bow-legs or the ref's need for turn of foot.

Back to me at school now. What about the discovery of books? I'm a writer today and words are things I fill myself with, head to toe, from stories to dreams.

The poet William Shenstone, Dr Johnson tells us, loved books so much that as a child he was happier and more likely to sleep if he had a the comfort of a book under his pillow, and that his parents could make him happy even with a wooden block in the shape of a book, used for that purpose. I know that kind of comfort very well. In my case, even before I could read, I hoarded the rich red-backed classics for children published by Dent. I adored their luxurious appeal well before their contents produced patterns of meanings and spurred my imagination.

Mine is the story of a boy who caught the rare but sadly addictive Shenstone disease, and never recovered. He is now beyond help and the condition has led to his pathetic habit of being lost in libraries and bookshops for hours, and to the sad plight of the confirmed reader who has to have words, and have them now. Even worse, the Shenstone disease leads to that plague of the bibliophile, the joy of feeling, stroking, staring at beautiful books even if their content is nothing more than a study of Chinese moths or the history of paper-manufacture in Britain.

This lovely, chaotic love in a working-class family with countless cousins, uncles and aunties across the city gave me the joy of family games, laughs, whimsicality and stories: but none of these from books. Our first proper house, inhabited after my parents had served their marital apprenticeship under the same roof as Grandma and Granddad Wade, was in Halton in north Leeds, in the suburbs, and was a tied house – tied to my father's job as a baker and grocer at the end of the street.

Here I furnished for myself a world of grand narratives, as a pre-literate word-child who could find prompts to his imagination in the stories found in comics, but only through the images. Until the age of 12, I could not read anything but the most rudimentary texts. I had the stories of cowboys and adventurers; explorers and astronauts, told in pictures in *Eagle*, *Victor* and *Film Fun*. There was also the wonderful baloney of Desperate Dan and Roger the Dodger in *Beano* and *Dandy*. But mostly, I spun my own stories and so there was no need to learn how to read books.

Of course, there were no books in the house. No Bible, no *Robinson Crusoe* or even *Pilgrim's Progress*. To my relatives, a 'book' was a word used of women's magazines. Hence, my mother asked for her book, *Woman's Weekly*, and that was the usual reading-matter of the household. There were no picture stories there. There was reading: the time for contact with print was Sunday morning. Dad would lie in bed for hours, eager for the scandal stories in *The News of the World* and *The People*. Mam read *Woman's Own*, which was then largely mumsy and predominantly about making jam tarts and knitting jumpers for Christmas presents. But the stories in the Sunday paper provided the powerful tales that sustained the imagination. Horrible murders, scandalous affairs, matters that would raise a disgusted tut and a smile of pleasure at the relish.

After all, this was in the days when hanging was in its last few years. Stories mentioned and talked about were of callous murders maybe not too far away from us in Dunhill Rise. Mam would read a crime report, then talk would wander on to stories of a murder at Beeston which she always remembered: the killing of Dr Dewar. She had been 17 at the time, and the doctor was killed in the driveway of number 176 Beeston Road. The killer, Thomas Richardson, was hanged in Armley Gaol, the castle prison towering over the streets where some of Mam's relatives lived. It was a story of adultery, like so many of the B-movies we watched: the doctor had a weakness for women, and his destiny was being battered with an axe in his own yard.

That was the reading in our house – dark deeds just around the corner or scandalous tales of the famous and infamous. But books and stories found me and I was trapped in their charms for life. Before I made up tales for the written word, I spoke them – to myself mainly.

My mind was all about epic stories: I gathered armies of dramatis personae from various military eras in popular narrative history: I had the requisite personnel for the Battle of the Little Big Horn, The War in the Desert with Montgomery, and the siege of the Alamo. Long before, in the age of tin soldiers, I had enacted the Boer War and the Zulu War, but the troops were now buried beneath the fertile soil of a Yorkshire village, having been given full military honours.

Round about 1957 the age of the plastic soldier arrived. I gathered mystical and enchanting packets of soldiers, some squat for cover; some charging the enemy lines, and others cowering behind artillery. I even had the officers. For the American Civil War I had huge numbers of the blue and the grey, some on horseback and some looking official and dictatorial in imperious stances of command.

My stories were oral. I filled the garden with deployed detachments and battalions of men. I moved across the grass and rockery, giving myself a dramatic commentary as a cannon wiped out a position in the hills or a breathless messenger arrived at Gettysburg to deliver the bad news.

This blissful pre-book microcosm went on, with my childish self having no idea of the imperial themes I was propagating. It went on until one day in the English class, my charismatic teacher read us all a story: read the novel aloud, and dramatised the whole thing. I was captured for ever by the spell of books: actual, physical, paper and cloth books you could hold and love and bring alive. The work in question was Nevil Shute's gripping tale of metal fatigue in aircraft, *No Highway*. My heart went out to poor, bumbling Mr Honey, who knew that the safest place in the plane was the toilet, and that the young stewardess he was smitten with should be persuaded to head there with the utmost speed. The teacher undoubtedly smashed all the golden rules of pedagogy. Today he would be ousted from his position for having given no attention to learning theories or lesson plans. He had created a totally passive class, doing nothing, but by God, we were churning inside with passion, expectancy and sheer magical enchantment that such a dull-looking book could spin such tales.

I went to the library and searched for the name Nevil Shute. There was nothing there with his name on the spine. But anything about planes would do, particularly if there was a chance that the huge craft might splatter apart any minute. I recall combing the shelves, finally settling for any cover image with the slightest hint of disaster at sea or in the air, and then giving up. But I was destined to take the first step to acquiring the Shenstone disease.

The problems were still there at school. I was hopeless in any subject involving maths, science or technical work. My attempts at making a poker failed miserably, despite my pleasure in hotting up the coke in the forge. I still had my stumpy finger sliding under the words, and I had to say every word or sound aloud, the frustration growing as I wanted to de-code the story quicker than I could take the next breath.

Nowhere could I find a copy of *No Highway*. But something told me that other books could be just as compelling if only you gave them a chance: who knows, they might even compete with my own versions of major battles in world history? It was then that I found a certain ripping-yarns author called Admiral Lord Mountevans, and his story of the Jacobites, *For the White Cockade*. Everyone must have a Shenstone book, and this was mine. It begins: 'The fading rays of the July sun were splintering themselves through the leafy branches of the trees of Glenfinnan as a shabbily-dressed lad paused in his ascent of the rocky glen....' Well, I struggled with 'ascent' but there was a lad there, and that was a good start. There was soon some bother on, as my Leeds Granddad would say, and I was in rapture.

This was a book to put under the pillow, even if you had read only two pages, and that with your finger under the words. The book had been responsible for a severe attack of the Shenstones. Everything about the book made it offer untold delights: the blue cover had a drawing of sporting accoutrements such as football boots and a fishing net; the dust-wrapper had bold Scots warriors in action, and the picture of the author looked authentic. Here was a chap who could spin a yarn.

I didn't put the soldiers away for ever, but I started to believe that there were other stories than my own, and that even metal fatigue could be interesting, as well as the white cockade. Our very unliterary secondary modern school, surrounded by the Teddy Boys and deeply engaged in telling imperial British history, might just hold some wordy treasures there somewhere, and the Admiral and Mr Shute had made me determined to find them. The only way to win here was to decode the words, and the struggle had begun.

This epiphany made no difference to my poor performance in the technical drawing class; nor did it enhance the skills involved in understanding and working out decimals and algebra. But it did stimulate me to see books as something more than comfort-pillows. In particular, it was the reading aloud by the marvellous Mr Makin. What I witnessed, as I now understand, was a piece of drama just as boyishly crazy and enmeshed in a grand story as my garden epics.

There would be no going back. I was Shenstoned and there was no help.

One match in the first phase of our league days was against a team with a reputation for class, and they had a striker who supposedly scored in every game. I determined that he wouldn't score against us. The game illustrates the tendency for Sunday commitment to go beyond all sane bounds. We were 2-0 up close to half time, then our best striker was limping. He had to go off. This was an irregular called Benny, but he had scored both goals. We would miss him. As he sat on the grass, writhing in pain, I noticed that people were saying 'Done his hamstring' and when I looked, his groin was black. The skin had turned black, as if mortified. People laughed, it was so bizarre.

Anyway, we had to hold on. It was 50 minutes of defending. About ten minutes from the end, their star was about to hit a pile-driver and I put my foot in his way. My instep received the pile-driver. We won 2-0 but I had my first injury. I recall that most of us walked off holding various muscles, and that socks were down and shin pads loose. We were all patting each other on the back, though, and I forgot about the pain. One thing the game proved: the 'Doc' was no use for groin injuries. He could only sort out your philosophical difficulties. It's worth the slap on the back and the reward of a smile of triumph, having that sore foot. That would change: a defeat would not. So, it was de feet that saved defeat, dare I say. Someone else said it – the team joker, a figure every footballer at every level will know well. We know the team jester from the template of Gascoigne maybe. I think in Revie's team it was Billy.

The Strip

Now, as members of the league, we paid subs and a proper kit appeared. The blue and white stripes were the Huddersfield or Sheffield Wednesday colours, approximately, and somehow, that magical thing happened: clothes actually changed attitudes. Anyone who has never donned a sports strip will not understand the amazing transformation in the mind when one moves from tatters and makeshift to the real thing. I know that I stole a peep in the mirror and this man in a new strip looked back like a pro, and then as I trotted out onto the grass, I felt something changing inside me. The rub of the nylon against your skin, the way your limbs are somehow enhanced and your sense of self grows into something quite pretentious – these are mysteries. All that may be said is that you feel as though you can perform better and that you have a duty to that strip – a duty to at least try to play up to Jackie Charlton's standards.

It brings to mind the Romanian team dyeing their hair blonde during the 1996 World Cup. It is tribal and clannish – the pack is showing off its identity and its togetherness, the fact that it's a unit despite the individuals like Georgi Hagi who clearly have skill beyond the norm. But even at park level, a real strip magically transmutes the mind and its attitudes. One mis-kick and you want to apologise to the shirt.

The league presence also meant that I felt the need to protect my legs more. I know that I used to pad the delicate bits with extra cardboard or wear extra socks. The shin-pads always slipped. But you were gearing up for battle, as it was clear that the referees were never able to spot the worst fouls. The absence of linesmen didn't help either. The thugs knew what they could get away with.

Changing Room Chat

Now the team mentality began to take over. We started quite well and had won most of our first games. The changing room gradually became a challenging, disturbing place. It was where a whole range of male identity found expression. It was in that sweaty, cold, forbidding place that various forms of Trial by Macho would take place. The weaker players (those who would not die for the team) were mercilessly ribbed, and the drinking prowess of the young bucks was manufactured into narratives of epic proportion. These are the rules of the changing room:

- Always join in when the victim is teased
- If you are the victim, smile as you are destroyed
- Never lose your cool or you will be teased to the point of suicide
- Make jokes about jock straps

- Never mention women
- If your woman is mentioned, do not defend her honour
- Always denigrate yourself
- Perfect a cynical laugh
- Adopt the team ideology – even if that means adopting nicknames
- Most of all, smile all the time, even when your cheeks ache.

The ritual of the changing room tended to comprise several phases: the arrival is full of stylised pack-marking: the good players are greeted and patted. Their sexual or bar-room habits are commented on. Then the stalwarts who have little skill but total allegiance to the team are greeted. This greeting is more jokey. Finally, the vulnerable ones creep in. They are welcomed with jeers. Most informative here is the status of the team comedian.

The comic works by sheer, bold vituperation. God help the man who misses a tackle or goes into dream-state when the striker is put clean through on goal. He becomes the scapegoat, acquires a nickname and is branded forever with the enormity of his error. The comic relentlessly reminds the victim of the one notable mistake, and every Sunday greeting will open with something like, 'Now then Lardarse, got your Brylcreem on? It might just give you that advantage when t'ball slips off your head.'

There seems to be a fixation with testicles in football. The Gazza image, as he is done by Vinnie Jones, is an icon to this bizarre ritual. What it shows is the triumph of hoodwinking the referee. The comic is a master of this, and it is the source of his power. He is the canny one who outwits authority. He can be relied on to entertain the troops by reminding them that authority is comical really, and that a foul is open to shifting definition.

For the sake of a documentary record, this is a typical piece of changing-room banter as if recorded:

"So you got permission then, Dennis old son?"

"Permission?"

"From her indoors."

Dennis had been let out as long as he's back by 12.30. 'Have you got a note, Dennis old pal?"

At this point Dennis attacks various bare backsides with the wet end of a bath-towel and the noise is so high that it upsets the legendary drinkers who are brooding in the dark corners.

The attention turns to Phil, a man who never spends money on football gear and who is notorious for being a cheapskate and looking naff.

"Hey Phil, you got cardboard in your boots again? Can't your mummy afford boots?"

(sniggers)

"Hey Phil, that a jock strap or a truss from your granddad?"

Phil now snaps and the comedian is dragged to the shower for a dose of ice-cold local authority water.

Touchline Chat

Some of the best conversations come about while walking the touchline when injured, and you're there to support the lads by shouting loudly and clapping till your hands smart. The normal scene is supposed to be an old man and a dog. But there may also be assorted eccentrics, crocked players who have the vicarious thrill of pretending they are playing. Their legs spasm with every kick and some develop stiff necks from the repeated imaginary heading of imaginary balls.

Most conversations with old-timers, crocked players and know-alls tend to be the kind where they say a million words and you nod. But there was one memorable chat I had with an old chap. He was tiny and wrinkled, full of homespun philosophy. He said, "You know lad...watching football, it's the parable of the talents." He gave me a close look, to be sure that I had some Biblical knowledge. I smiled so he carried on.

"Yes, that's why it's a wonderful sport. Each man has a certain talent. Some are stoppers, some are good headers, some can beat a player... you know, so they all use their talents and work together. Like a real community. That's why football is always going to be there, big in life, you see. The main reason being that even the slow 'uns (here he looked at me) and the ones who are just cloggers, they'll have a place, just like they do in life."

I asked him to go on. He had me interested.

"Well, it's like when there was a war on. We all needed to feel we belonged together, that everybody could work at what they could do, and then you put all that together and there you go, look out Hitler, watch out Kaiser Bill."

I remember thinking that school history lessons had never been like this. He pressed on with his thesis.

"Right, so like an army, or better, like a village, because real football is about village teams. None of this big-business stuff. See, it was conceived to show that a community could win against all odds, and that all bits worked together like a well-oiled engine."

He was like some professor, I came to think. He was an amateur pundit of course, but he gave me the sense that he was somebody with an interesting background.

"Now you see son, do you know a film called *The Quiet Man*?"

By this time I was paying more attention to him than to the game. I nodded. "John Wayne."

"Right... now see, Brits are quiet men. They walk around with nothing to say, they can't court women properly because they have no conversation, but put 'em on a footy pitch, and they become articulate... listen to 'em shouting now!"

He had a point. I was going to ask him a question but he was ready for going and he turned away. "Nice talking to you, lad."

I had to find out who he was, and I asked if he was a player, or if he'd been involved in the local league.

He turned, smiled broadly, and said, "No lad, I've been a milkman all my life!"

Tackles, Injuries and Excuses

North Kinley took tentative steps in the first years. The 1977-80 period was marked by the relentless progress of commitment and its demands. Training was announced, discussed and discarded. But we did manage to have official representatives at the committee meetings, mainly to keep an eye on the opposition and to socialise a bit in the best Lincolnshire pubs. Rumour was that the reps were only there for the real ale.

Gradually, though, we strengthened the squad and had the luxury of substitutes. But this was counteracted by the frequency of injuries. Every Sunday would see the line of semi-cripples or walking wounded. These minor bumps and strains were the result of clumsiness rather than malevolence in most cases, though there were notorious thugs in some teams and due preparation was made for these encounters. I always had my own categories of tackle and resulting injuries. First was the tackle clumsy as a cart horse. This was standing on the player's foot or body-checking him. Second came the tackle violent: this was a simple chop that sent the player into a dive to earth. Finally, there was the tackle Very Naughty, which was only one stroke away from a Hospital Job. A Very Naughty meant a nasty slide or tackle from behind which would cause a wound or bruise that would last for the next three weeks.

A Hospital Job was hated by all, and only the few psychos in the league were capable of that. They had adopted the Vinnie Jones philosophy that winning was all that mattered and skill was a waste of time. Chopping the enemy was the only view to take. After all, it's a man's game and so on. There was always an excuse.

But how do we learn the difference between a fair tackle done with expertise and a vicious hack? After all, in my generation, football skills were rarely taught. School was kick-and-rush and the league in Leeds had been learning by experience. You watched the good players, then practised, in a desultory way, on your own. In my case, the basics had been learned in the all-day park game which took place on the Gipton Estate in Leeds. Each side would have anything from 20 to 25 players (men and boys) and subs would be made as players had to go home for tea or household tasks. The games ended at dusk, and scores were often 23-41 or similar. Gipton, if you drive through it now from the York Road, is largely boarded up; it's had the drug problem dig in deep and you sense the disenchantment running in the blood of every soul treading its streets. But in 1967 the playing field was Eden – timeless, joyful, men and boys and dogs together, thinking of nothing but beating the man in front or smashing in a shot past the two keepers on the line (the real keeper and his assistant).

The point is, I did my learning there. Every game would have its balance of really clever, dextrous players who could feint and shimmy, do long balls and swerving shots. Anyone walking past could shout, 'Any game?' and would be allotted a team. In that way, patterns of play changed as the day progressed, and the moderate observers (like me) saw all variations of attacking play, defensive agility and anticipation, and midfield control. I came to see how you were supposed to beat a man, how a tackle had to be made after attaining a certain pace, and how positional sense made the difference between success and failure. In fact, I've always had the feeling that some very powerful players joined in, some who were playing with top local teams.

With that inheritance, in the Sunday league in Lincolnshire, I was ready to accept my limitations and play to my strengths. But injuries were inevitable. The commonest were black eyes and bruises of course, but the team had its share of broken legs and concussion. In my case, it was more a feeling that my brain was turning to jelly. Heading a football so often and so many times leaves you with a headache. Mine used to last until Tuesday evening. That was so even when the heading was done by the book, with the big bones at the front of the head. But there would always be desperate times in a match when either the ball had to be taken on the side of the head, or I was just thumped when my head was in the way of a drive.

Injuries were also less observable ones. My foot was painful all the time for months, but I was fooled into thinking

I had recovered until I actually put my boots on, then it was excruciating. This brings me to the question of pride. Male pride is inextricably linked to injury. I was expected to play on with a limp after a bad kick, and I also had to bear the laughs when a ball hit me in the goolies and I writhed on the turf for several minutes trying to be tough, when in truth the pain was like a particularly nagging and acute form of torture, as if irons were gripping your tenderest parts and all you could do was grimace and pretend to smile. Usually I played on, covering the torment with a bluff manly exterior. This exterior is part of the overall performance. One chink of fear through the armour of the macho code and bingo – the changing room becomes your hell.

This 'playing the game' in spite of everything is what leads to the famous cases of men playing on with broken ankles or necks. The Bert Trautman experience is well known to many park players. My most vivid memory was of a game in 1980 when I had fallen on a frosty pitch, slamming into the creases of knife-thin earth with my chin and mouth. For a week I had a broad red patch of bloody wound which made me seem like a victim of a mugging. The day after receiving this, I had to give a talk at the University over in Hull and I gave a grovelling apology for my appearance. There were uncomfortable winces and coos of sympathy from the ladies present.

This working-class macho is apparent everywhere on the park. The really telling moment is this one, a case study in high farce:

> Phase one: player receives sickening kick to shin. He holds the wound. Trainer sprints on with the 'magic spray' and cold water.

> Phase two: player limps and a few desultory claps arise from opposition and meagre crowd.

> Phase three: player attempts a jog back to position, all eyes on him, and for that silent 30 seconds, the player's heart bursts with pride. Then later, when alone, he shifts between tears and smiles.

1977: General Studies

When North Kinley emerged as a force to be reckoned with in Division Two (as long as the key players were sober), college began to be more interesting, as I started to notice players from the opposition teams in my classes. I was teaching on a very ambitious programme of General Studies at this time, and the apprentices were expected to spend an hour a week absorbing history and culture. About this time, I selected my subject and explained it to the Thick Plate engineers. I had decided on hieroglyphics. After all, General Studies could be anything. If it grabbed the students' interest, then go ahead and do it. Lecturers looked at the master syllabus and then schemed to find a niche for whatever they knew and enjoyed teaching.

Of all the options – trade unions, lives of the engineers, basic law and so on – I selected my favourites and devised interesting activities. When I first put a board full of Egyptian ideographs and pictograms on the board, I was met with the familiar cry from the heart of all artisans in such a situation: "What the fuck has this to do with plate-laying?" I was usually lost for an answer, but nevertheless, talked for an hour, and by week three they gave in and were settling down to translating hieroglyphs into English. To add some spice, I made all the English sentences statements about football. This only served to remind one young man, a square-shaped type who mended tractors for a hobby and who played for one of the village teams, that I was someone who had marked him once.

"Hey, you're that tosser who kicked me. I'm gonna chop you next time, old pal!"

I don't know whether this rapport helped or hindered the learning process, but it was absurd. We moved on then to debates, and I know that 1977 was also the year in which I discussed the question, 'What is the point of work?' with a class of painters and decorators. By week three, we had agreed that work is actually more necessary than leisure. One paper-hanger became totally preoccupied with the Socratic Method and said he had tried it on his mates. The result was another changing-room torment. I was stunned and impressed that he had grasped it: he was adept at taking a question and pushing it to an extreme, always asking why until some new thinking emerged.

The team began to notice, after the second season ended in a creditable place, just outside the promotion spot, that women were beginning to come and watch. Girlfriends brimming with curiosity and not wanting to be left out would come and ask questions in between the ridicule. Sometimes a young wife would bring a baby and pram or pushchair and loiter by the goals. One kind soul actually started making sandwiches, but that was discouraged as unmanly. A suck on an orange was considered refreshment enough. The real hard cases would even decline that and spend half-time doing press-ups.

The first North Kinley team. Note the palatial changing room and the lack of a consistent strip. Second from right, back row, was a guest German player, sadly not called Beckenbauer

But also at this time, the female element became more of an issue. It was noticed by the tactician and the midfield general that certain players were always out late on Saturday and had clearly been busy in bed when they should have been sleeping, conserving energy for the Big Match. This caused ongoing banter often directed to wives and girlfriends involving threats of financial penalties, and eventually it was mooted that anyone arriving 'shagged out' took the kit home for washing. Washing kit had become the bane of our lives now. There was supposed to be a rota, but the canny ones always had bribes or excuses and the married men ended up taking the stuff home.

Excuses

The Sunday park player is a specialist in excuses. The main variety is the one explaining the 'freak goal' that was not his fault. My own favourite was 'I was marking the danger man...' thus implying that Dennis and not me should have been taking care of the scorer. But you were expected to nod sagely when a player excused his lack of speed with 'On the piss last night'. This was more acceptable than 'Missed training' or 'It's my injury still troubling me.'

The excuse needs to be inventive. Being in a competitive game forced no end of innovative lies on players. My notebook lists these as the most egregious but just plausible excuses for bad play:

- I was just distracted by that kid's yell...
- I'm on nights and I can't get the right sleep
- He got first run on me
- The referee/linesman was asleep
- Why the f... do we play the offside trap?
- I normally play on the right
- There was an explosion in the street.

But the most impressive excuses are those given in explanation of defeat. After one horrendous 5-0 thrashing, the pub dissection of failure pointed clearly at the defence (which included me) and their dreaminess. The charge was 'Ball-watching' and the normal excuse is stress. But my offering was more concerned with passing the buck and blaming midfield. The credo of each position is, 'You can't attack/defend/play midfield without the support of a good attack/defence/midfield.'

I can recall that after that game I came the closest to murder ever in my life. I walked past a sort of filthy dugout in which the victorious enemy were gloating. The gentleman in me said, "Well played" and they sniggered. My fist went hard into a wall, wanting to smash a jawbone really, and only my teacher's self-control stopped a brawl or a premature death of some young footballer from the carrot-cruncher land (they were a team from an isolated village).

The basic idea of this wonderful, nonsensical, absurd game is that excuses are pathetic and only make you look weak and daft. But still blokes went on making them. If a ref got to know one of these types he would see that the guy was giving him some mouth, and even before he read his lips or heard a word, he would guess the excuse. One player specialised in obscure medical excuses. The ref would say, 'What is it this time – delirium tremens?'

'Yes ref, how did you know that – you a quack then?'

The Old Enemy

By our third season, we had established which teams you feared, which you could just manage and which were poor. We had an arch enemy: a bunch of country lads calling themselves Bannow Castle. This lot were natural mud and boot players. Their habitat was a barren wasteland beyond the end of England, into that Grimsby hinterland which has been forgotten by the world and remains in its pristine state of elemental nature. When we played Bannow Castle, it was to win. We all knew each other very well by the third season, and they were our most serious promotion rivals.

We had beaten them 2-1 on our home pitch, and the return was out in the wilds. I feel sure that every park player will know the feeling. As we made our way out in the minibus, everyone knew that this was a grudge match, because they felt we had beaten them with the help of a poor referee (a bent referee in their eyes). In my case, I knew that I would be marking their six foot four striker. I am five foot nine. I knew that I jumped better for the ball than he did, but the problem was he always bent into me or pulled me down.

I had my personal challenge then. We all had a sense of foreboding. Imagine the scene: ten o'clock on a misty sharp morning by the Humber. The village had not stirred. Bannow were ready and agile, bouncing about the pitch warming up. Our lot were mostly hung over. The kit was mucky again after a quarrel about the washing rota. Pete had the runs and had to knock at a door asking to use the loo. He was told to go away. So as the referee called us in and blew the whistle, John was retching on the touchline and Pete was looking for a toilet.

Bannow scored after a minute. A wind blew and a knot of carrot-crunchers gathered to scream abuse at us. Things deteriorated when a speculative cross beat our goalie, who was trying to look into the sun (they had even won the toss and given us the dazzle-end).

We lost 5-0. I remember trudging off, dejected, with my head throbbing, the last man off the pitch, and I saw the line of Bannow players smiling at me. I congratulated them on their impressive performance with the normal, "Well played Castle!" And this was received with sniggers and mutterings of ridicule.

Dad would have considered them as unworthy to play the game.

Challenges in the Classroom

Parallel to this confrontation was the learner teacher's nightmare. I had a problem class. Now, difficult classes are usually angry, noisy, disruptive and a real pain to teach. This class, a group of laboratory technicians, never spoke to me. Week after week went by. I was teaching them the history of British trade unions, and trying to initiate debate. My questions were met with silence. I would constantly try to prise open the speech mechanisms of the most affable faces:

"Chris – how did the skilled artisans educate themselves in politics?"

Blank face. He looked at someone else and shrugged. I made countless attempts to ask questions and have some kind of response, but the faces were unmoved. Not a sigh or a grunt emerged from them.

Even worse, a man at the back was a player-manager of one of the league teams. I had seen him applying a sponge or moaning about a refereeing decision. I tried the ploy of talking to him quietly, after the class, but he coughed and hurried off.

I broached the subject in the staff common room, asking the experienced old professional, a dear friend (an ex-trialist for Preston North End) who gave me some sound advice:

"Tony, I have this class, and I'm having trouble."

"Well I always said you could come to me, Steve. What's up? They throwing paper aeroplanes about?"

"No, they won't speak to me."

"Well that's not a problem, that's a blessing from God. Let them write essays and you do some marking."

"No, I mean, it's weird. They never say one word – at all."

He was gob-struck.

Then, one Sunday, the man with the sponge came over to talk to me at half-time.

"It's not you, Wadey – it's General Studies. They're boycotting the subject. They see it as a waste of time. Just give 'em a quiz about chemistry."

It worked.

1980 also brought my first experience of teaching foreign students, and this was on the steelworks. There was trouble at the time, in the aftermath of a row in the town in 1974 about language tests which were legally required under the new Health and Safety Act. Of course, there had been a certain antagonism to testing steelworks employees and the word 'discrimination' had been used with reference to the Council for Racial Equality. But by the 1980s, it was accepted that tests were really for the benefit of everyone.

The French teacher and myself were asked to devise tests for the foreign workers on the plant whose English was not so good. Obviously, they were a safety risk around the blast furnace if they couldn't read notices. So there I was in a small Nissen hut bordered on one side by the huge rod mill and on the other by a railway line, teaching a mixed bunch of workers how to read basic English. Luckily most were football fans. I abandoned the hieroglyphs and got them talking about their teams. The two Italians had no problems, but I had reached a brick wall as far as the Middle Eastern men were concerned. The only sport they liked was chess.

But I used the old-fashioned method of repeat and learn, and soon we were all saying:

Leeds United are the Pride of Yorkshire

so that it made the metal walls reverberate. It had its perks. The two Italians brought me massive bottles of Martini to show their appreciation. The Ukrainian, Stefan, told me the real history of the struggle against Hitler and Stalin; a scholarly looking man who always wore a suit, shirt and tie told me about walking past a door in his native town in India with 'E M Forster' on the door. "He taught me, the dear old chap. Mr Forster the novelist. He taught me." This guy wanted to make every lesson a cultural dialogue between myself and him, ignoring the rest of the class. He would ask me if I thought the novel as an art-form was dead and I tried to explain the silent 'b' in doubt to the beginners. By the time I came out and started walking home, I was talking to myself and wondering what it was all about.

I was told the story of the last shift by one of the foremen. It was his friend Peter's last shift. Peter had had some kind of bad news, some family problem, and had always been very quiet. On this particular shift, he had been particularly broody and difficult. Then, after the shift and the mass exodus from the works, time passed and Peter had not arrived home. His wife rang. People looked for him. The police reported that there was just one car left all alone at the far end of the car park. It was Peter's car. He was never found, and the foreman was sure his friend had gone into the furnace-mouth.

Myself in a Leeds United shirt, on holiday and pretending to be the great Jimmy Greenhof, whom I looked a bit like - or so I persuaded myself

"Right in there – another lump of impurities – or slag. Happen we all become slag eventually!" His joke was strained.

As the class progressed, I got to know the Ukrainian very well. This was Stefan Czupil, with whom I've now lost touch, but I owe him a great deal. He was the first man from Mitteleuropa I ever talked to with any depth. In fact, I never fully sorted out his story, but in essence, this is my poem for him, and it defines my interest and his deep sadness, because he was truly a melancholy man, whose only pleasures at that time seemed to be talking about his daughter and rolling a cigarette as slim as a spruce tree twig.

Misplaced Person

I was in Italy.
We don't be took prisoner of war
By British army. By German army.
Our own country was a baby of Russia now.
We were put as Misplaced Persons.
For two years it was,
And they didn't know where to put us.

They put badges on back of knee
And behind you. It was like clown.
P.O.W. And the same on trousers.
We didn't been fighting since then
But Hitler said, 'Will you fight Russia?'
'Will you untie your land's wrists?'
Nobody couldn't take us.
THEY didn't want us and THEY didn't want us...

Now, if you go home,
You not Polish any more.
We've had the box-wagon life,
We've had the life scything in the wheat.

Every time I bent in the wheat,
I pretended the gold there was home,
But looking at the skies, well...
They were English clouds.

I can hear Stefan's voice now, rasping or soothing, always with a poetic quality fused with his broken English and his Polish thinking. It was from Stefan that I first learned about the Polish football team. "They do not do no well at all, you know why Steve? Because they argue... like schoolboys. They don't like the shirts... what do they do, sulk. They don't like the manager's brand of cigarette... they sulk. Never do nothing, Polska team, Steve."

Revie's Leeds Heroes 3

Paul Madeley

Madeley was, to my young eyes, all muscle and shine: the kind of player who you just know is a superb athlete. Ask any Leeds fan what defines him in the chronicles though, and they will say, 'He played anywhere.' I'm not sure when and where the term 'utility player' crept into common use in the football press, but I suppose he was that, and yet it seems to belittle him as well. Why? Because he was so smooth and easy with his skill. A Madeley goal was a very rare thing, but you didn't mind that. You could depend on Paul Madeley. It must have taken some guile and determination for an opposition player to get round those thighs. He was solid.

One memorable event in the Madeley story was that he said no to Sir Alf Ramsay. He had the chance to go with the team to Mexico but didn't. There is no doubt about the fact, because he has explained why. He wrote in a 1970 memoir: 'I looked at it this way: I was not a regular member of the England team...

In fact, I reckoned that if I were not among the original 40, I was extremely unlikely to get a game, if I did go to Mexico. And that's a long, long way to go for nothing.' He did eventually clock up 24 England caps, though.

He was also 'mentally and physically whacked' as he said. Paul was such a reserved, humble type. When he learned that Revie had valued him at a quarter of a million pounds, all he could say was that he wondered what Bremner and Hunter must be worth. There was always an air of gentlemanly good breeding and right thinking about him. In an old reference work from the 1940s, a comment made about Leeds was: 'The man who signs for Leeds United must be a good player and a good citizen: he must be a man who will uphold the dignity of the professional football player.' That could have been written for Paul. But he stood out in many ways. In the team photo for the 1964-65 season, there he stands on the back row, the tallest of the seven men, his solid shoulders sloping down to rub against Jimmy Greenhoff at one side and Terry Cooper at the other.

He was six feet tall but looked bigger, and weighed 12 stones 5 lbs in that year, and he was Leeds born, rising through Leeds school and Farsley Celtic, and then being a youth international by 1962. He first turned out for Leeds against Manchester City in 1964. He played in two cup-ties against Everton, and in one of these I was squashed in the crowd and lost, feeling almost asphyxiated.

From 1966 he was a regular player, and highlights have to be the Fairs Cup game against Juventus when he scored the away goal (1971) and in 1968 he had first started to wear the number 8 striker's shirt, as he did in the notable thrashing of Ferencvaros in 1968 with a score of 4-1. At the height of Leeds' success, in 1969-1970, he played a major part in the winning of the Fairs Cup and the League Championship.

As the man of all positions on the field, he could be relied on to step in, as he did when injuries struck – maybe most dramatically when took Cooper's position after the number 3 broke his leg, in the 1972 FA Cup Final. Leeds won that 1-0 – surely their most frequent score-line.

My memories of him are similar to my memories of the great John Charles – in the sense that he was a broad-shouldered player, excellent in the air, and always likely to have his opponent bounce off him as both climbed for a cross. How to evaluate him is a riddle. In 1968, when he played against Arsenal in the FA Cup Final, the comment was that, as usual, he had never played in goal for Leeds, but had played in all other positions. A better assessment was given in 1974, when, as champions, the players were all summed up. The writer noted: 'Paul Madeley, to use an old footballing expression, is a footballers' footballer. He can be quietly unobtrusive – then suddenly burst into action with thrilling acceleration that takes him out of the quiet middle-of-the-field zones in to the heart of penalty area action.' Of all his roles, he liked midfield best.

Paul Madeley must have tired of being described as 'the most versatile player in the English game', but on the other hand, it marked him out as special, and that's tough in football in any respect.

4

Organisation

Back in Leeds, in the Revie days, my Dad had taken me one night to watch Leeds beat Ferencvaros 4-1 in the Fairs Cup. After the game, he took me to the Prospect pub in Hunslet and there, through a crowd of drinkers, he pointed out Jack Charlton. Jack was eating a pork pie and had a frothy pint of bitter in front of him. This was a revelation to me. I had the myth that professional players had strict regimes; that their bodies were temples, and special diets played a part in their success.

My notion was that this was all down to being properly organised. I thought that Don Revie and Les Cocker, the coach, would be so in charge that spies would rush out and stop Jack from eating that pork pie.

"Dad ... it'll ruin his game."

"What? Beer?"

"Well, the pie – fat and all that."

"Nay lad, look at this then." He opened the *Yorkshire Evening Post* and there was a feature explaining why 'Storming' Norman Hunter was so hard in the tackle. It was all, it said, down to his landlady feeding him Yorkshire pud and full breakfasts.

"You can eat what you like lad, if it gets burned off." My Dad's words had stuck with me. Now, in this Sunday league, I had a phase in which I thought our team had a lack of organisation. But I couldn't do much about that. Training never really happened, so I determined to train myself. It didn't work.

First I tried running, but my lungs rasped in the cold air and I just developed a stitch. Then I tried a rowing machine. This caused muscle pains in my chest. I cut down on beer and walked a lot. But somehow, I always seemed to find somebody faster than me, and I used to battle for breath after a sprint. My mate at work told me the obvious.

"It's your pipe. Smoking ruins your fitness."

I haven't mentioned this yet, but you may have just gathered I smoked a pipe. I looked stupid. The seventies me was hairy on top, hairy above the lips and shrouded in Whisky Flake tobacco fumes. On top of that I expected to be fit. But I stopped worrying when I realised that most players in the league were the same. Little knots of desperate smokers would take a last drag of a snout before jogging onto the turf. Our star striker was clean as a whistle, but the character players were famously debauched, playing after filling every bodily tissue with beer the night before.

There was a crisis meeting after a particular defeat and it was suggested that we make a real effort to train. I think we gathered once, and Alan, who was supposed to be experienced in these things, explained a few moves, stretches and training devices. I just came home stiff and sore.

But organisation went deeper. It was also about responsibility. Someone had to collect the dues, buy a new ball, go to meetings or apply discipline. What we needed was a test case, something to see if we were together or not. It came when a player was fined. Nobody was really sure what it was he had done, but it did involve abusing the referee and walking off the pitch in disgust. I think he had shouted abuse for the rest of the game, and the official had had enough. He was reported to the Committee. The fine was £18 I think, and we were all asked if we could chip in and help with the fine. The first response was to agree and money was handed over, but brooding, unhappy asides were delivered making it clear that the culprit had let the side down and was a prima donna.

Still, every team needs its colourful characters. Ours was temperamental and capricious, apt to desert us if the mood took him. The main cause of this was being kicked repeatedly. He would walk off if this had happened too often, and he would say "This is not bloody football" as he exited.

The thing about fitness and training is that there is always the injury, and on the park that invites high drama. The best dramatists on the pitch made a knock into something from opera. They'd pull a face like a clown, writhe about in agony, accept a cup of water on the face and then get on their feet and carry on. But the point is that they always have an excuse. I can't move this foot... I can't see clearly.... My arm is stiff.... That's all very well, but I've known excuses that pertain to nothing but sheer vanity and nonsense such as 'My hair gets in the way' or 'I have a blind spot' or 'I've had flat feet since I was a nipper.'

The topic of flat feet is odd indeed. I had flat feet , and only found out after the school nurse sent me home with a letter. Mam and Dad looked at me and tutted. I always thought that flat feet were an advantage if you wanted a career as a copper. But anyway I had to go for special exercises, with my feet wiggling up a wall-bar rung or being pressed into more orthodox positions by a brute in uniform who had wanted to manage the Olympic team but never made it and so took out the frustration on school kids. Me and my flat feet carried on playing footy anyway and it never seemed to stop me running. Maybe I ran like a duck, but nobody told me if I did.

Promotion for North Kinley

The year 1981 saw us in Division One and there must have been a celebration of some kind but it is all a blur. The season had been eventful; new expertise had been absorbed, such as the heading-off-the-line ploy, and the pack-the-goal-area technique. But there we were, with new blood and a new striker who was reputed to be Graham Taylor's nephew, scoring regularly and showing some neat twists and turns. Of course, we had stiffer opposition now, and the summer before the opening game was swollen with rhetoric and the hubbub of expectancy. But 1981 also saw Scunthorpe suffer a severe blow. The massive Normanby Park plant was to close and a depression set in across the town.

At college, the result of this was phenomenal. We had a flood of people hungry for qualifications and a launch into a second career. The normal September enrolment was swollen to gargantuan proportions. Suddenly, I was contemplating English classes of over 25 mature students, all keen to read poetry or even Shakespeare if it would get them a piece of paper with the word 'certificate' on it. I had never known such rapt attention in the classroom. They would have had no problem with the hieroglyphic if it had GCE written on the top of a sheet of official-looking paper.

Of course, we had all been affected in some way by the steel strike in January 1980. It was all about money and something else – the shaping of the whole industry. There had been a massive world-wide slump in the trade, of course. Scunthorpe had been huge: a plant covering 3,350 acres, with 256 miles of railway. The strike, when it came, stretched to 13 weeks and eventually Normanby Park works closed.

Anyone who has not experienced it would have some difficulty imagining the effects of a massive closure on a one-industry town. Scunthorpe had had the boom years, and had known a phase of being a rough place of shifting labour, temporary housing for workers and ethnic identity. Now it had to get to know a stranger: unemployment. Normanby Park works had been a broad expanse of high metal frames and structures like an alien landscape, something the family saw on a drive out to Normanby Hall country house on a Sunday excursion.

Now that was gone, and a mental shift took place in the town. Droves of people gave everything in adapting to what business guru Charles Handy has since called the necessary portfolio work of the capitalist economy; the skills they had were fine only if there was a steel industry. Tell the workers from the sinter plant or the slag processes about portfolio work. I found myself trying to do something else – teach them Shakespeare, commas and the imagery of poetry.

So I had questions fired at me every day. Students who actually wanted to know more sat in lines, hanging on every word. They asked for books to read. Another thing they did – the young men – was join football teams. The Saturday league burgeoned. Every park seemed to overflow with noise and colour at weekends. Leisure was becoming an industry. There was one young man who epitomised the tough, deep, defiant quality of steel people. He was an archer in his spare time. I saw him firing arrows the length of his thin garden into a huge target board. He wrote about archery in such a way that you knew he had made it part of how he defined life.

Another student, Graham Randall, wrote about the end of Normanby Park and his life as he saw it then; it was published in the arts magazine for Lincolnshire, *Proof*, which I was editing at the time. Graham wrote about the last day: 'I pulled myself out of my own gloomy thoughts and started to walk up the mill. The air seemed to hang heavy about my head; there were a few more things missing that day. I touched a guard rail which bordered a machine; it was deathly cold ...'

It was Graham's essay that made me see that I should teach creative writing. But in the meantime, I had to push and shove these rows of sad but hopeful people through some exams.

The Dossier

I compiled a secret dossier on all the teams we played, and I am sure that none of my team mates ever knew about this. But I enjoyed logging the various teams and their characters. Looking back, it seems that they were all as over-confident as we were, and paid the price! But it was always fun, and football provided a rare thing: a total escape away from stress. No-one used the word 'stress' in 1981, although there was plenty of it about. But football was surely stress therapy par excellence. Here is the dossier. Those park players reading this might recognise their own team.

The Hospital XI

A smart outfit, but like us, subject to regulars being well below fitness. They play with a basic plan of the high ball and a nippy midfield. One bloke carps a lot and niggles at you, playing a mind game of his own invention.

The Buffs

These are quite fast for a not-so-young outfit. They talk a lot to each other and wear you down with their sheer sense of life. But they lack basic skill.

Boughton

They are the invincibles, winning every match with ease. Brimming with confidence. You have to man-mark tightly, and they have a powerhouse play-maker who needs to be stopped.

Polish Club

No Poles here! No continental style finesse, but true grit. They could be the Wimbledon of the league. All blood and fire, dash and feint, promising great things but not really delivering.

So it goes on, a set of rough notes, singling out the danger men and spotting weaknesses. It kept me amused. Still the season in Division One had only just begun when I had my first piece of literary glory and I was playing the Libyans when it happened. If it is subject to a modern spin, then this tale is counted as an international match. We had Libyans at the college for a few years and they challenged us to a game. Just as this was about to happen, I was still editing *Proof*. The photographer came, his job to take a picture of me for the front cover. He was later than expected and instead of me being in a sober book-lined office, I was on the pitch, facing a fast and talented striker who was trying to exhibit my shortcomings as a man-marker to the crowd of mostly Libyan supporters.

Gaddafi's men were here for some kind of engineering training, but all I could learn was that it was to do with valves. They were a happy shower, always smiling, but this day, with the score at 1-1, I was called over to the touchline and made ready for the photo. The team yelled at me to get back on, as we were under siege. But just as someone was taking a throw-in and there was a lull, the photographer snapped me. A Libyan behind rushed up to him and demanded to know whether he had been in the picture or so I thought. The journalist who was there thought the man was a criminal. His English was poor.

It turned out that he wanted to buy the camera. But in the fracas, they hit a post and I was dragged back on. A month later the magazine arrived: Wade smiling on the cover, spattered in mud and in footy gear. Every inch the literary man, in the grand tradition of Albert Camus, goalie for Algeria. I don't think it advanced my literary career, but it was a neat twist, taking football out of its anti-art/culture image.

The crowd had a few of the new late developers from Normanby, and I recall that one mature lady said my playing style was like Sir John Falstaff's might have been (he was the fat knight and she was implying I needed some training, I think.)

I smiled at her and quoted: "He lards the lean earth as he doth walk along..." But we all shook hands and so ended our only international game. The spoils were divided.

I now had two allegiances. My teaching job was a profession, of course, and I was learning the trade: I had acquired a PGCE in 1976 and was now established on the staff. But I had also discovered a transformation in myself that in a way reverted to type, revisiting that teenager in the Leeds teams. I now saw something deeper in all this park football; what it does is magically transmute dross to gold.

I realised this after we lost a game to a freak goal. The opposition were nothing special and we were not playing well. It was destined to be a 0-0 draw when a little man with gap teeth and thinning hair leapt for a speculative header which looped high over us and into the net. A few weeks later I saw that goal-scorer, ambling along a street, looking completely ordinary, even grey. He wore bland colours and just walked with his head down. How could that game metamorphose that plain man into the scorer of the winning goal ? Well, it did and does, and always will.

I was in the business of transforming all these ranks of newly unemployed as well. The year went by with a host of new relationships; I made friends. Most of the students from Normanby were my age or older. I came to see just what rich lives people led, beyond their workplace, and that my subject, English literature, was something of a puzzle to them. I came to know Robert, a bubbly, imaginative young married man who asked questions like a philosopher. He kept pushing me for an explanation of why people spent their time analysing texts.

"Why call them texts anyway?"

"Well, it just covers all the different kinds of, well, texts."

"But I read just to relax. Why search for all these meanings?"

"Because it opens up other lives to us."

"Hmm... do I want to cope with more than the one I got... that's a puzzle, mate."

He went away to think, and I knew he would be back. It was strange at that time, switching from intellectual, explaining about poetic imagery, and then switching to stopper/sweeper mode. Going from mind to body in such extreme ways made me rethink my father's life. After all, he had done the same, playing for Churwell FC for years after the war, until he sustained a serious injury. Something happened to his arm – a problem with a joint and some nerve tissue. He was advised to stop. It went down hard.

I know that he was the one responsible for this park passion; I started to think about him. He had died while I was away at college in Wales, and he had written letters to me. These were full of a sensitivity I had never been aware of in his speech and revealed a man who was good at making relationships. But the other thing the letters showed was to what extent football, at least to a northerner, is a metaphor for art. It actually replaces the aesthetic impulse in the serious books and 'Culture' with another code of beauty. This one is all about style. There is no other word that covers it.

I know that when I watched our team play, the really natural, graceful, stylish players stood out like warriors in a farmyard. Playing the game totally, with every inch of you and with your mind and spirit, that was the secret. My father had understood that, and he expressed it in the way he talked about John Charles, for instance.

"Do you remember John Charles as he went majestically up the middle of the pitch? Just dominated it, went like a strong horse, a gallop to the line; nothing could stop him hey? Great stuff, son!"

I saw John Charles on television not long ago, receiving a

degree from a Yorkshire university. The muscles, the solidity, the manly decency and stalwart nature were there still, the soul of the footballer. Even more heartening, I saw it on the pitch in the meanest Sunday game in the regional league. A man who had this style had it so it shone out of him, all the time, even when he was watching the ball at the other end of the pitch. Now he's gone. It's hard to believe.

Leeds United Heroes 4

Ronnie Hilton

You don't actually have to be a player to go down in the annals of Leeds United history and distinction.

What true Leeds fan could ever forget the most naff team song ever: Ronnie Hilton's , with its wonderful refrain of:

Ronnie is best known for his classic rendering of and . He had the same Brylcreemed charm of my Dad and of most men of his generation who aspired to wear a suit and sport a tie with a strictly regimented Windsor knot.

As Ronnie was forever linked to Leeds United, it should be noted that he was born in Hull in 1926, just one month before my Dad. But he had nine Top 20 hits whereas my dad just sang in the bath, his speciality being a song about an orphan fly: '.' We wept through many a Christmas with that. We also filled up with emotion singing about our pals at Elland Road. Again, like my Dad, he went away to have a go at Hitler and came back to Leeds to find himself in a new world – one in which he worked as a fitter in a Leeds sewing plant. He was doing that while my Dad travelled around the suburbs in a Co-op van selling groceries.

Yet again, the Calypso was not naff at the time. You sang it and you felt good. You wanted to think that Big Jack,

Gareth and Billy were indeed your pals. In fact, Ronnie recorded several football anthems, helping that genre to achieve new highs in compelling lyrics and emotional thrust. These included (1964), followed by the best and the strong-surviving and in 1970. Still happy to work a successful seam, Ronnie had two more recordings, and . Later we had as well, and it must seemed that the appetite for tribute songs was bottomless.

Ronnie reached the top, with chart singles on his CV from 1954 to 1965; he even appeared on the Morecambe and Wise Show, and fortunately he failed to win a place representing the UK in the first Eurovision Song Contest of 1957. Of course, Revie is Mr Leeds United but if you had to suggest an equivalent form of address for a non-player then it might be Ronnie Hilton as Mr Terraces Sing Song.

He died in 2001 and surely goes down as one of the greatest personalities behind the media clean-up of the Leeds image, when the fans were gathering a reputation (undeserved) of being mindless thugs. Hopefully people will recall Ronnie's songs more than they will the shameful ripping-out of seats at the infamous match with Derby County.

Still today, when he see his name or his picture, I start singing to myself the words .' Ronnie, we love you but you have a lot to answer for.

Under Scrutiny

Christmas came, and North Kinley were mid-table. But the new students were shooting up the league. In the literature class we were through our first progress test and the mature students were scaring the younger ones with their marks as well as their enthusiasm. I know that one session involved some acting. I asked Mary, a lady of mature years, to 'become' Mistress Quickly and to talk about Falstaff. The character is a 'bawd' in the Boar's Head tavern. Falstaff is a gross and witty customer who entertains everyone. He is in debt but survives with his unlimited charm. Mary did us proud. She switched off her normal self and was Mistress Quickly. She gave answers from her instinct, not her student-brain preparing for an examination.

That was how I wanted North Kinley to play, just slipping into the right role. But what I had come to see was just how many mental elements there are in success on the pitch. Confidence can ebb and flow at will. We had an important Christmas match at Brigg. If we came away with a point, we kept fourth place. Then there had been cup matches and we had been deteriorating, losing form. The confidence was ebbing fast. We started well, and withstood some early pressure. They had a few near misses; we were adequate but no more. Then, I remember thinking how close we were to being a shambles. Our goalie kept yelling out, "Talk to each other. Let me hear some calling!"

Someone in the crowd began shouting at the keeper to encourage him. He made a good save, taking a low ball on a wet pitch. The voice behind said something like 'Well taken, keeper. Great save!' and I felt something rise – in all of us. It was a feeling that spoke and gave a hint of being able to find some confidence again. I can bring to mind that kind of change inside; it's like changing gear in a car when it's been rumbling in low gear and at last has a transition to a smooth running-over, doing 'hot miles' on a long stretch. That feeling on the pitch is what changes a game. It starts with one player sometimes, as when a sub comes on and makes a superb saving tackle, giving heart to all the others.

The Brigg team thought they were on a winner, but the game stuck at 2-2 and we came off with a moral victory. I know that a Brigg player said, "You got legs like iron, Wadey..." and I felt almost as if my father were inhabiting my skin. He used to say his thick legs were his best attribute, and then chuckle.

North Kinley started the new year in a creditable position. The students came back lusting for success. I could feel something in the air in Scunthorpe, some kind of will to escape. People had been talking about the depressed state of things, and how closures somehow close down people as well, and a desperate chain reaction sets in. Yet, my own little classroom appeared to me to represent King Canute, ordering the tide of depression back.

The league was expanding now. New teams were arriving in Division Two. We determined to try harder, and soon the phenomenon of the 'Ringer' entered my consciousness. I knew that in horse racing, there had been cases where a trainer had substituted a Derby horse for a hack in a selling plate if the two horses had been physically remarkably similar, but the ringer in Sunday league football is a comical case-study in the psychology of the game. A guest player signs in, if he is not on your registered list of club players. Johan Cruyff could have guested for us if his beard was long enough and the sky was dark, so he couldn't be recognised.

Basically, I suspect all clubs did it. But we came to have a penchant for it. One day a German cousin of a player arrived and played for us. It was like watching Best in an old Third Division game. I think he signed in as 'David Smith' or something, and as long as he never spoke, we were fine. The odd thing is that ringers stood out like sore thumbs, they were so overflowing with silky skills and made things look too easy. A canny manager would place him in a shady part of the defence where he wasn't noticed, then let him come out in forays and score with a drive from 40 yards.

Ringers brought the real spectacle to the game, like when a ball had been cleared and bobbled past the half-way line, to be collected by a guest player and chipped in from distance, just floating into the top corner between post and upright as if measured with a slide rule. Another occasion was when a ringer was a brother of a regular player and they were so alike, even our own team became confused and called out the wrong name. Once you have a top-notch ringer, the hard part is keeping him sweet. You make sure that he doesn't buy his own drinks after the match; you wash his kit, and you laugh at his jokes.

June came and the usual hot examination weather. I patrolled the aisles, watching my mature students write for their dear lives. I had never known such a clamour for extra sheets and note-paper. They all left the hall with hard calluses on their fingers and nervous smiles. I remember that someone collapsed in the hall and went into a fit. I grabbed them and held them up, gripping under the arms, and after that I had no idea. One of the students was a nurse and took over.

Once more, I thought, how good it was to do things with the body as well as the mind. The endless English Literature talk was making me question things, but also making me value the Sunday league even more. 1981 had been a great year so far.

5

Training?

Notice that this is a question, not a fact of life for the Sunday player. We often talked about it. I think once three of us turned up in mid week, ran the length of a pitch and then went down to the Comet for a swift half. On the whole, training is not a part of the park footballer's scheme of things. He has more worrying topics loitering in the recesses of his mind. Questions such as Bass or Tetley's? Questions such as Liverpool or Everton? It was always enough just to say the word, have a chuckle or a snigger in response, and then carry on drinking.

But down at the technical college it was becoming a mite serious. I began to notice that paper was breeding paper at an alarming rate and that there was a broody, uneasy resentment creeping into the General Studies classes. It was something to do with training as opposed to a Liberal Education. We die-hard humanities guys with a gospel of free verse and Marxism for the masses were bothered by this growing sullenness in the classes which were once seen as a 'doss' or a 'laugh' but worth doing because it made you think. Now there was open defiance. It came to a head with the Ag Mechs, the Agricultural Mechanics.

These ten young men encased in dried mud were on the whole quite happy to escape the wet fields and bogs to ogle young ladies and drink tea. But unfortunately everything was now part of the Master Plan for Liberal Education. In teaching there is a Master Plan every term. One after another tends to gather a vocabulary, some acolytes and a wad of paper to back it up. Then it dies away in a cloud of serious essays in learned journals and the next one comes along. This one involved a complete education in the liberal arts of the Middle Ages with some ancient history thrown in, and a module on the history of shipping because that was the passion of the man who devised this particular Master Plan.

I was supposed to 'train' these Ag Mechs in, I think, the ability to analyse and interpret tabular information. I knew it was never going to work because at the first meeting a guy with legs as long as the Pennines, said "I ent doin no fucking writin."

This was a red rag to a bull. I negotiated. By week three, I discovered that they had to pass an examination involving writing some sentences about tractors. We did spelling. In fact, I devised as many ingenious spelling tests as there were brands of tractors on the market. In the end, we had a laugh.

But 'Training' was an issue. It was the time when the government wanted to differentiate between 'teachers' or 'lecturers' and 'trainers'. Now I had worked alongside, and played football alongside, some great guys who knew all about engines or joints in carpentry and never once did I think that my degrees made me any better or deserving of a different status. So the row raged on.

In the end, someone gave in. We could get back to the football and the re-education of the Normanby Park workers. But all this fuss made me evaluate what exactly I was teaching. My huge English GCE groups were happy to find out why such topics as Keats and Dickens were so highly rated, and generally they ended by agreeing that these reputations were justified. But my thinking led me to some fantastic experiences. What shows the excitement of this is a course in which some plasterers and decorators were supposed to be following the Master Plan into the area of trade union history. Instead, I asked them what beauty was.

"Well ... women's bodies."

"A nice rounded bum."

We moved from this to such knotty topics as a green leaf in spring or a baby's finger. But most agreed that it was hard to define. So we set about defining other tough words. By week six we were dipping paint brushes in philosophy and the Amalgamated Society of Engineers would have to wait.

On the pitch, with unemployment in the town now at around 19 percent (this was 1983) we were gathering strength and winning more than we lost. The general pattern of a game was that the defence would hold everything with a mix of desperation and marking; the midfield would run around and get in everyone's way, and the strikers (who were pretty hot) stuck the goals in. Against two or three teams who took it all a tad seriously we lost 2-0 or 2-1. But we were up there in the top five.

As we improved a little, the pub talks raised the level of analysis from 'you slow bugger' to 'I know... let's pass the ball to someone with the same colour shirt on as us!' and so we felt that snug camaraderie of the huddle, although even the thought of a pre-match huddle back in those days would have sent shivers of fear up the spine of the toughest centre back.

The only problem we had was with a keeper. We had lost our first one, a former hockey goalie as mobile as the Grand Canyon, and now we were always trawling mates of mates to have the odd game. One day there was a rumour that the goalie who turned up was a semi-pro. He played magnificently, and made me realise how unfit I was. That was the turning point. I would start a personal quest for fitness and speed. I bought cheap shorts and a hiking jacket and started to run the streets late in the evening. At first my lungs were apparently made of cardboard, but with a bag of brass tacks rattling about in them. I would stop, battle for an intake of breath, and avoid being seen if possible, keeping to unlit paths and shadowy streets. Then it improved and all the spittle came out of me; the beer belly wasted away, and I sweated so many impurities you could have polluted Australia with it all.

It was a good time to do daft things like that. The reason being that I was finishing a course, doing extra marking, and teaching around 26 hours a week. You needed something to kick or you might have kicked one of the bosses.

The gospel of Training also meant that more teachers started to suit up and look flash. There were odd words creeping in – words like 'seminar' and 'conference'. Then there were the business gurus. Proper young teachers just had to be seen carrying a handbook with a title like 'Make Your First Words the Killer Punch' or 'Clinch the Deal and be Liked'. It was only a matter of time before the 'student' was replaced by the 'client' and a group of students were destined to become a 'cohort.'

So there was more and more aggression to be loosed on the park. But the team was still in the cup as the rounds went on in 1983, and we were actually through to the semi-finals. There was one team thrashing everyone, and if we got through the semi-finals, then we would surely play them. They were Broughton and they were a useful lot.

But I remember a terrible story in the middle of all this; there was a student whose wife had walked out – not left him for someone else – just left the house and started walking into the country. Scunthorpe is like that. In a few minutes you can be away from the Westcliff estate and into open fields. Or you can walk up the hill beyond Bottesford and be in rural Lincolnshire in minutes. A neighbour had seen her walk out, and it had been while the student was in my evening class. By the time he was home, she had had three hours in which to walk, and she could have gone in any direction.

We were full of awful talk. Someone recalled a time in the Thirties when he had seen a ghost – a headless woman walking in the fields near Burringham. We all dreaded that this student's wife would be found dead. It seemed like suicide – or a state of despair that might lead to that. There had been many stories of suicide in the papers at this time – after all, we had fought a war, had huge national strikes, and shrunk major industries down from bellows to whispers.

She came back. The wife walked back into the house, staring around like a hunted thing. It seems stupid to say this now, but I know that I felt a shiver of pleasure as the student said to me: "She looked like Ophelia in Hamlet, Steve." This man had been reading the Bard from cover to cover – a man who had only previously read motor-bike magazines and porno. But once he struggled through *Henry IV Part One* he wanted more and went away with a vocation.

I hope it helped him understand his poor wife. There was certainly no 'Training' any teacher or college could give him to cope with this. He said to me a line from a song: "*Life is too short to cry...*"

There had been some rough times in this town but people were coming through. The year 1975, for instance, brought an explosion at the Queen Victoria furnace and there were 11 killed. You carry on. The team goes on, my Dad would have said. But for the time being, the big question of the day was:

Would a flash of brilliance from Baz get us into the final?

Remember Baz? Marxist, chemist, incessant talker, beer-shifter of mighty capacity; all-round good bloke who knew every line in every *Phil Silvers Show*. We needed a special goal from him, or even one from the poacher, Ken. Yes, there was this feeling that we COULD do it, and throw off failure just this once... look out Broughton.

I devised my own rules for 'Training' one day while doodling at a dull meeting about assessment criteria. I'd been upset by a discussion about what to call those students who were 'Special Needs.' They had been given various tags since I had been in education: the most dodgy I ever heard was 'Compensatory target groups' but we also had terms far more questionable than I had experienced at my secondary school in Leeds where they were 'The Remove.' Anyway, this was my list:

Training is for dogs, not people

Training is obsessive

Training is loco

Training has a nauseous vocabulary that makes me puke.

That was a watershed for me. I decided to defend my high ideals about teaching – nebulous maybe, and concocted from dreamy romantic poeticising when I was a shop assistant in Leeds. But I was going to do it – keep teaching poetry to the plumbers when I should have been doing the history of banking.

As for the town at that time: well, in 1980 coke-making at

Redbourn was packed in; Normanby Park coke ovens were turned off, and the last of Redbourn's blast furnaces was smashed. People talk of a special camaraderie among the Redbourn works – one not really found at Appleby-Frodingham some say. At that time, often when a workplace closed down, what was lost was something that could not be quantified like the business capital: it was the enjoyment and satisfaction of doing work that spilled over into community and friendships, into the Gala and into Sunday sport and drinking sessions. It was 1981 when Normanby Park closed for good. Our team was steaming away, finding form not long before the 1984 National Union of Mineworker strike and then the shifting of everything into a new identity as Scunthorpe BSC.

The Semi

Well, the game was fought out in puddles and there was a ruckus about whether we should play the offside trap. The forwards thought we should, and the defence thought we were too slow to make it work. Personally, I hated the idea. So we did what we usually did – scream at each other to mark anything that moved – sometimes even the odd stray dog. After all, offside was a concept as far beyond comprehension as astrophysics. I know that I had spent hours in my Subbuteo-obsessive days debating offside, and the definition changed. Although to be fair, 'interfering with play' in that context more often involved a beer glass on the pitch than anything to do with football.

The opposition were slick alright; they were cocky as they had beaten us in the league. But my moment had come, and it was to leave me with a sore foot for the next month. Our best striker, Ken, had given us a one-goal lead and there was about ten minutes left. The striker for the enemy was about to crack a shot at goal on the edge of the box when I just managed to get my foot between the ball and his upper. The result – a lump on my foot but a one-nil win.

Strange, but I can't recall the celebration; just my sore foot. I know that Ken had a groin strain and that it had turned black again. Someone thought he had the pox. "No, it always turns black when Ken gets kicked there... genetic," Baz said.

'Bring on Broughton...' was the cry.

In class, I had been having some success with English as a Second Language by writing about the history of steelmaking in Scunthorpe. We had made drawings of blast furnaces and lists of key dates. In one session I had real difficulties in explaining why accidents happened so often. I had them all hanging on my every word when I told them about a man who had fallen from a roof when he was painting it, and he had dropped down into a pan of hot slag. A man tried to pull him out, grabbing his leg, but just the boot was taken out. Nothing else of him was there.

We had fun with the history. I told them about the famous Four Queens – the blast furnaces which had that name since 1939. A Middle Eastern gentleman, from the Yemen I think, was well informed about some English words, and led the discussion into why 'poofs' are called 'queens' and we had to take out a dictionary and so the lesson folded into that familiar chaos known by every ESL teacher in which varying moral standpoints are questioned.

The session ended in a friendly argument in which one Asian man denigrated another's wife for smoking. "The woman who smokes ... very bad lady ... very bad lady ... not allowed at my house."

But that didn't matter to the quiet man at the back, who told me for the umpteenth time, "I saw E M Forster. There was his name... on the door."

One student never got past A B C and smiled every week, apologising for his bad memory. We said Ah Be Ke so many times, when he saw me in town ever after that he shook hands and said, "Hello Ah be ke... you well?"

Four weeks from the final of the President's Shield, to be played at the ground of Brigg Town, and I was training by pounding the streets, cutting down on beer consumption, and heading the ball against the garage. But I had known failure or at least mediocrity since the Rose Forgrove days, and I was anything but sanguine about our chances. And yet ... there was a sort of omen.

It was one night, as I stood out the back of the house, looking up at the heavens. There were the usual stars and the odd red-tinged cloud above the steelworks. But then, there were these three oval-shaped things, going across the sky, directly north, in unison, and they were moving in a staggered way, darting and then stopping for a split second. Never before had I seen a UFO. I had drunk just one glass of beer.

I willed it to be one. I even said a sort of Yorkshireman's prayer to the spirit of Don Revie. I think I brought in my other hero, John Donne, as well. Now there was a guy who could get inside any knickers on offer, so you bet your last bent tanner he could fix this one, and open up a defence.

6

Tactics: More than Kick and Rush

Being out of work eats at you, slowly and insidiously. I was workless for several months in Leeds back in 1966, but then I was young and waiting for the right break. But to be in your fifties and in a steel town, then out of work, that's a different matter. In Scunthorpe hordes of men took the redundancy pay and thought that, in spite of everything, there was a buffer state called 'lump sum' and tomorrow could wait. But the damage done is there inside. It's about waiting and there is a long corridor with rows of chairs, and you might just be able to make out a little door in the distance with 'Interviews' written on it, scribbled on a rag of flipchart paper.

It was as if there was a lead weight on the town. I imagined the Greek view of the Gods, up there on Olympus, toying with us. I could see Zeus smiling as he put a massive rock of depression on top of the steelworks. There, let them be glum. We needed some other God to fight our corner – someone like Orus the God of Ironstone or Stella the God of Steel, to chip in and lift the thing off us.

Out of work, you drift. It's a midfielder when the long ball game misses you out. You spend most of the game craning up to see the ball up in the light, on the way to someone else.

I wrote in my journal at the time about this and I called it Doletown. Now I see that I was writing as an outsider, a visitor from Yorkshire, and more than that, a pen-pusher, an intellectual. I was like the poet, Douglas Dunn in his book *Terry Street*, playing Radio 3 while he tried to understand the natives. But there was a difference, and dare I say it, I was born working class and had carried this odd, perverse guilt in me. This is totally insane, but working-class blokes with chips on their shoulders usually order them from Harry Ramsden and let the taste and smell linger there all their lives.

Pathetic. It's a waste of a life. But on the pitch, I met and talked to real Scunthonians, people who actually worked on The Works. I had a little experience. I had once been out to a place called the Sinter Plant to do a language test. For hours on end, a steady stream of young Asian men sprinkled with a white dust came in and smiled at me, before repeating some ridiculous English that no-one ever spoke anywhere. But again, it was all cultivating my sense of doing something, doing more than that sympathetic cluck you do when you meet someone in deep crap.

People had different tactics to cope. A game plan, like any other, can have surprise results. Some relied on the Pools. Others went down the bookies. More level-headed folk enquired about sorting out a moderate stash for later on in this perilous journey. Scunthorpe is a family town, traditionally; when steel was big here, as in 1967, 25,000 out of a population of 71,000 were employed in the industry. It is also a steady place. Kerouac would have loved it – for half an hour at least before moving on.

One day I was walking behind two workers who were in town to do shopfitting. One said to the other, "Eh, it's a laidback town this, innit?" He had it in one. If you want to drive over the middle of the road here, you're off the motorway for good. After the slump, there were suicides. That was another option. As I write this, I can see the top of a tall tower block. Three or four poor souls chucked themselves off that. And that was more than just losing four-nil to some pub team.

But it is generally laidback. The extreme cases end up in a mess. I had a student in this period whose main tactic in life was to follow Blackburn Rovers. That was enough for him. He was a trainee electrician and used to come to my class, in a hut, with his RAF greatcoat and long blue and white scarf. He wanted to talk football, not write good sentences. The problem was he had very poor ability with English. I talked to him, and I saw that he was lonely, that there was a rift in his family.

I tended to cover his essays with lots of red pen (frowned upon now) and then we would laugh about it as I went through the spelling rules and tried to make punctuation fun. I have a clear memory of making all 30 lads snigger with the old chestnut about commas: the letter to the trenches in the Great War from the wife to her soldier husband:

'Not getting any better, come home...'

and then they have to re-position the comma.

"Ah, 'not getting any, better come home'... clever that Sir!"

But Jim was more glum than ever, and he was missing for a few weeks. Then he would appear again. One week they had done a test and I collected the papers in. That weekend I covered his script with the usual red pen. The next Thursday I was told that he had hanged himself in his room. Why?

"It was over a girl, sir."

He had loved from afar, never saying a word to this woman, and then ended his life when he saw her with another man.

That is not a good tactic and it's why, I realised, you need the team, and you need to drink together.

The team did plenty of that as the final came near. Never before had I understood the psychology of park football as well as I did at that time. The surface of the talk was about how good the opposition were. The first phase was all linked to the humour of defeat. Then there was a shift into 'Hang on, let's take this seriously' and then laughter again. Finally we had, 'We can beat this lot ...' I wonder if Accrington Stanley carry on like that before a cup draw with the Arsenal?

The fascinating workings of being shunned were in action again. No park team has a concept of 'squads' or 'reserves' really. It's a case of a group decision about these factors:

Who's likely to be sober on the day?

Will ......do a suicidal pass-back?

Who would not be prepared to die for the cause?

Whose missis will insist on no celebration after the match?

Anyone who popped a toe in the water and didn't like it was suspect. It was to be total commitment. Motivation on these occasions is done by what I call the Your Round Threat. The drinking session goes on, and you buy your round. Then it's your turn again but you promised to be home by two, and anyway, there was that long talk with the wife about sorting the household budget now there's no work and...

'My round... sure. Same again, Ron.'

Tactics in the college were now all about qualifications. Staff were being told that it would be useful for their 'career profile' to have a certain 'trajectory' in mind for their professional development. It was a time when departments changed names. There would be tiresome meetings about whether a section was to be a 'faculty' or 'school' or even a 'division'. In the mid-eighties I first noted the split between the die-hard chalk-facers and the suits. These were the normal characteristics, and I have faces from memory in my mind as I write this:

Revie's Leeds Heroes 5

Big Jack

Now it's all Barbour jackets and fishermen's pants, and not long ago, before he got fed up of being a pundit, it was the usual big-gob assessment and strong opinions. But the point is that Big Jack was so respected that you accepted what could be seen as bullying and bias as a part of a huge personality. My first memories of him are of a towering figure, with a neck that would have cracked the post if he crashed into it.

Jack Charlton, from a famous North East football dynasty, was in my blood for sure. In my Dad's school football autograph book, there's a picture of Jackie Milburn, tough and strong, fearless in the tackle, but a gentleman. The Milburns were the Charlton's uncles, and three of them had played for Leeds earlier in the century.

Big Jack was the kind of player that any forward would have dreaded in a collision, and when a gaggle of tall men went up for a cross from a corner, Jack would be the one that the others would crack as if hitting steel. It must have been down to the pork pies and the beer. But then, on a personal note, I have to say that he can claim status as honorary Tyke in the same way that I discovered, after doing some family history, that I have Gateshead blood and claim status as an honorary Geordie. For years I had expressed pissed-off attitudes about, as Geordies invaded the territory of this iconic Yorkshire soap, and then one day I found that I had ancestors called Fishwick, from Gateshead, and other Wades from Teeside as well.

I think it must have been Big Jack's Geordie bellowing that put whalebone in the corsets of the Leeds defence: not that they needed corsets I assume. But maybe they sneaked in an extra shin-pad when playing the Old Enemy Manchester United or (earlier) the Yorkie Enemy, Huddersfield Town. It's easy to imagine Big Jack calling you shameful names if you refused to back out of a tackle or you dreamed for a second of the post-match pint of Tetley's. He moved easily, his long legs covering ground smoothly and his knees up like a hurdler. He was always there to stop a fancy-pants dribbler and clearly hated himself for any shoddy play.

You could see that he was manager material, because you always felt that he could shake the nerves of anybody who was not up for the fight, and without swearing if in the public eye. God knows what language emerged in the dressing-room when the Newcastle dialect was let loose.

If Big Jack's head collided with a post, the post would crack, not his head. Anyone watching him play would have applied Stalin's nickname to him: 'Man of Steel'.

Chalk-facer

He or she reads *The Guardian* and worries about Guatemala. Their talk is of the Test Match, the game at Old Trafford, or the new biography of Isambard Kingdom Brunel. Fashion to them means the same jacket with worn elbows and the same cotton trousers with bulging knees. Teaching methods depend on lots of talk and a love of following a digression until it comes home again. Lesson plan is basically 'hold them until five to and then give them the nod.'

Chalk-facer questionnaire:

What is good teaching?

Helping people to think.

How do you assess work?

By assessing the whole person.

Is discipline a problem?

Only my lack of it.....

Suit

The suit has a need for ritual. He has to have (a) dark suit and loud tie (b) leather briefcase (c) Filofax (d) a portfolio of sample memos and a manual about handling official meetings. The suit pats you on the back, calls you Harry even if it's Frank; the suit pretends to follow Chelsea but thinks that a striker is a steelworker causing bother in the street. The suit wants an MBA more than a night in downtown Amsterdam with a new plastic credit card. The suit dreams of being a HOD (Head of Department) and of coining a new word for 'Meeting.' Hence the proliferation of memos about the next 'Thinktank' or 'brainstorming' or 'planning panel' in the college. At some point in one of these gatherings, the suit will flaunt the one football fact – something like good old Peter Storey scoring that winner at Wembley in 1972. He's said this a thousand times, so it is a fact, and it's bound to annoy me.

Suit questionnaire:

What is good teaching?

A well-prepared session geared to set learning objectives.

How do you assess work?

With reference to agreed marking criteria.

Is discipline a problem?

Not if you use it well and keep a lid on things.

The best teaching tactic I ever heard was from a wise old teacher called Denis Bowden, who told me: 'You can loosen off, but you can't tighten up. So start off tight with 'em lad.' This was spoken by a man who specialised in a hard stare and a meaningful silence to impose order in class. He taught history by anecdote, such as his tale of the WEA lecture on Keynesian economics given by a local teacher one time, and when he finished he asked for questions. A man at the back stood up and said, 'I have a question... My name is John Maynard Keynes.'

Students remembered Mr Bowden's lessons.

Out in the streets though, 1983 was a hard year. There had been the first flush of confused idleness and redundancy wads, and the aftermath was sinking in. Nothing going on. Who was going to make something happen? Everyone talked about re-training. Right, so you had your basic certificate, now what?

But the first hurdle was the exam, and my English classes filled the great hall, lined up ready to write about Falstaff and iambic pentameter. The feeling I had as I walked the aisles was like some weird paternalistic figure who had guided a horde of blind people through a minefield. At first the day was going well; I saw feet tapping and lips mumbling sounds. They were scanning. The invigilator from Maths thought they had all lost it and looked concerned. "Just working out pentameter," I whispered.

No sooner had I said this when I noticed that a woman had got to her feet and scuttled across the room, heading out of the place, and with no reason given. I had to follow her, as that was the rule. The invigilator must accompany a candidate who leaves the room, and be observant. I was dutiful but worried. The woman spluttered something that sounded like 'period' so I kept my distance. Unless you've ever invigilated an exam, you won't know the difficulties involved in trying to guess who's cheating and who is actually ill. If this was a ruse to gain time or crib an answer written on a sleeve, then there was nothing I could do. Was it a tactic to escape certain failure? The older teachers looked the other way, fumbled with sheets of paper or walked an aisle imperiously.

The tactic of having a fit to escape one's doom is not to be recommended. But neither is pulling a muscle out running when there is a cup final coming. I spent hours bending about like the India Rubber Man and then tried Deep Heat. I could never let the team down; that was instilled in the Leeds working man from the day he left his nappy behind. When you fell and cracked your head it was 'Footballers don't cry...' On the pitch, the best equivalent was when someone, heading off the line or tearing towards goal and missing the ball, thumped into a post and had to spend the week nursing a red lump the size of an apple, ridiculed by every green-overalled apprentice from dawn till dusk.

Tactics have always been related to philosophy. For instance, say you lost what you thought had been a 'job for life' at the age of 25; or say the girl you made into your Beatrice and put on a pedestal was seen with another man; or even imagine that the town you lived in was shrinking and instead of work there were bits of coloured paper with long words and promises on them. How would you rethink things? No-one usually tells you how to do that thinking. Well, now, thousands of qualified suits appeared from the dark forests of Training to help you.

There were rooms with names like Jobtalk, Workspot, Do Something Different and so on. Life was always about change, that's what defines it. But the first words go deep. A striker is not a centre forward, and a half-back knew which half he was expected to operate in. This was a fact that went profoundly into Scunthorpe's sense of being, as it would with any place built on one huge industry. You knew your place. You did your minute part of the task and left other skills to others.

This is where history and football meet: my father, for instance, turning out for the school team, turning out for the job against Hitler, then turning out for Churwell WMC. When you were a part of the whole but the whole thing needed your part, then things went well.

So unemployment means that after you have drifted and lost focus, and had enough of measuring out your life with coffee spoons or pints, then you'll open up in desperation to any attractive new idea – unless it's called Jobstart or Workboard etc. Okay, so you're asking the full-back to play striker ... well, we can try it, once.

In the rows of desks in the classroom, it was odd at first. The desks and chairs were all meant for kids. That meant every aisle in the classrooms was decorated with long legs in jeans; the big men and the tall men were trying to fit into the little rooms, as if they were outgrowing their lives. Scunthorpe had shrunk from a frontier town with horizons in a partition in an office block. People became visible in new ways, and they didn't like being watched. They wanted to do some watching.

But the results were excellent. They were the best ever so far in my ten-year career. I had always had this feeling that they would be special, that year of GCE students: they had given it everything, moving from 'Why doesn't Shakespeare write in English?' to great questions like, 'So you say he learned from Marlowe... what exactly did he learn?' Some of the students who had sussed out complicated things like motor-car engines expected poetry to yield up its knowledge in the same way.

A striker strikes

A fitter fits

A poem should damned well scan right and no glitches please.

I sank a few pints when the results came out. There were so many people smiling with a sense of achievement – people who had never found themselves at school and just taken the first and nearest option in life. They had done the hard work. I had encouraged, poked questions at them, and tried to smile a lot.

This was the first time, just before the final in Brigg, that I saw what football meant to men like my Dad. I could see why he took care with his glossy autograph book, adding comments and quotes. He used to write the obvious, but with style, such as 'A Charlton Athletic Player' next to a cigarette card picture. I started to put football into poems – something I'd avoided since my first scribblings when I was nineteen:

Visions of John Charles

Me dad. He played left back for Churwell WMC
Stylish sweeper or cursing clogger?
Never knew which, except the certainty
That his Brylcreemed black hair and knife-edge parting
And the broad shoulders, these were John Charles.

Broad as a Yankee road, he ran into infinity
Across the Elland Road pitch, midget defenders
Wriggling in his wake on the wet turf.

Yes, saw me dad's dreams in his face
Every time he got stuck in, and had visions
Of Wembley and a million hats in the air.
His tackles hard, but considered fair.

7

Those who Watch and Wait

There's a whole team in reserve as well, and I think of the women mainly. Back in Yorkshire in my Dad's generation, the kit was simple and spacious, and it was washed. I wince to think of the technology: a wash tub, posser and scrubbing board. My Grandma Wade was a strong woman with a workout like that.

But the women in Scunthorpe had been liberated. Some of these were the same blood as the women who had operated cranes, grabbed tongs and pulled steel plates, and cleaned out locomotives, when the men were mostly away at war. In the eighties, the only fair way to maintain any dignity and reduce the Sunday morning smells was to have a rota. Whether wives were paid I don't know. But when men had done the washing themselves, you had to be careful.

With single men, it was a case of high-risk exposure to unclassified bacteria. A typical Sunday in the changing rooms when, say, Peter had supposedly done the washing would mean that the bin bag would be taken from the boot of his car, where it had been since the previous Sunday, thrown across the concrete floor and then the contents strewn in front of the assembled players. The stink was intolerable. There would be a conversation like this:

My son Paul, treacherous in his Man Utd strip. He now supports Huddersfield Town and so has avoided the sad nostalgia of the Leeds supporter

"Pete for Christ's sake ... there's something alive in this sock."

"Pete ... I can smell Baz's cock in these shorts. You're supposed to fucking wash 'em ..."

"Yeah well, I got busy."

The guy's knowledge of Baz's cock was never questioned, you notice. Nothing queer about Carruthers, he plays footy.

Only Sunday park players know the hell of having to wear these unwashed, sweat-stained garments, with last week's mud clinging to them. There could have been anything lurking there: blood, snot and even tears. Somewhere in the heap of rank cotton there might be a jock strap or a few Elastoplasts or bandages; one by one they were tossed around, each man looking for his size, or maybe his own smell, then there was a chance he could avoid contracting the deadly lurgy in that bag.

"It's either wear these or no game." This was the player-manager, the Italian ace striker, Nico. "See ... this is not Serie A ..."

"It's not even fucking Unibond second reserves ... and we're playing in a cup final next week?"

It was on occasions like this that some would refuse subs. We paid a few quid a week ostensibly to pay the washing and mending costs and the referee, I think. But that was always grudging. The result was that every Sunday after the game, there would be a clamour and a firm demand that one of the steady wives clean the kit. The married men would then insist that Julie or Susan would not do it twice till the rota was through. So it went on, week in, week out.

But the supporting characters in the league were a floor-show in themselves. We never had a trainer, just a spray and a few oranges. But some clubs had a man who knew some First Aid; they even had managers who shouted instructions. When you played any outfit that took it all too seriously you had these animal noises all through the game:

'Chop the bastard...'

'Ref ... you're a fucking disgrace.'

'Talk to each other. Talk ... fucking talk ...'

'Bob ... you're not asking for it ... ask for the ball!'

There was one man who clearly thought he was Jack Charlton and Alf Ramsey in one. He dressed in that particular kind of Crombie favoured by the flash gits who have cigars the length of Chile and egos as fat as Billy Bunter. But this one was the smooth professional type. You could overhear him sometimes, saying something like this on the touchline at half time:

'See, there's too much space in that corridor ... move in behind the ball, then break ... but keep your shape ... you remember the classic Liverpool shut-the-door stuff ... well, we're a goal up, so shut the door and frustrate this lot. They're less than average and the striker's too old ... Think lads, use the old noddle, right?'

He was a natural for *Eastenders* and I've put him into fiction on more than one occasion.

The crowds of women who were, by this time as Thatcher showed the way forward, 'kicking some ass', are part of that Northern breed that do the child-rearing, the clap behind the head, and the caring support all in one; this is far too much for any man, and so we start by fearing it, move to a position of resentment and inadequacy, and then finally admire it but refuse to say so. This was seen in a classic example in the Second World War, when the women were so efficient at scrubbing out the engines on the works that the men turned sullen and complained to the union. The women were 'spoiling the job' – which means that it was supposed to be hard and manly and testing their skills and strength, and along come some women and show the men up. I ask you! There are stories of men loitering in dark corners to avoid having to talk to these Superwomen, for fear of having to say 'Well done.'

This Fight Hitler spirit was maintained through the tough redundancy times and was applied to anything competitive; it might be the daughter's dancing class or the lad at Cubs. If it was pride in the football team, then so be it. This was the breed of woman you wanted. It meant no more rank, stewed and obnoxious shorts, scraping your delicate parts as you put them on with a frown and a grimace of disgust. What it meant was, regular cleaning and more self-respect. When it came to washing kit, they would tackle anything except a jock strap. I think jock straps were sprayed from a distance, with Jeyes fluid.

People don't realise how important the appearance is in sport. A smart kit often means pretentious sods who look like nannies, but at a deeper level, it affects the mind, the attitude. You feel like a better man in a good strip, clean and shiny. There is a theory that certain colours are an advantage, suggesting power to the enemy. When our team first started we were just playing friendlies and the generally agreed colour was blue. If you had anything vaguely blue, you found a place on your body to cover up on a Sunday. Hence, the team photo from around 1978 shows about three out of 11 wearing the same kit; the others have either a blue shirt and red shorts or a red top and blue tracksuit pants. We look like the Clowns Eleven from Chipperfield's Circus.

But in the league it was different. We still had blue, but now it was all the same design. This was professionalism of the highest order. I recall that my legs felt thicker, swelling with muscle, and my chest four inches broader with that kit on. It was classy with a sense of tradition behind it, as in Sheffield Wednesday, and for three weeks it looked like what it was. Then the rot set in and some makeshift gear was spirited in. But overall, we looked the part, even if some mornings we had to be turned in the right direction and told which way to kick when the whistle blew.

Back in Leeds in the 1960s the Sunday League crowds were usually the obligatory three men and a dog. The only change was when there was a grudge match. One team in particular always managed to call out reserve spectators when they played us. I think the managing director of their firm dipped into the petty cash to pay rentacrowd thugs to stand on the touchline and abuse us.

One game was crucially important for them because a win would have saved them dropping to a lower division. Sure enough, as we got changed we could hear the crowd gathering. I remember that it was at the time when I lost three toe-nails after wearing the small boots again. I foolishly bought another pair of Woolworth's boots as I was strapped for cash. The result was loose toe-nails and a visit to the chiropodist again. I was a regular there for months.

This Sunday I felt the pain. I wrapped a bandage around the toes and still hobbled. I was supposed to be the nippy winger, and so when I started a run, not only did I feel the agony of the toes, but I also felt the hatred of the crowd. It seemed as if they were yelling in my right lug. One time the ball came at me square in front, so I headed it on and sprinted after it. The ball kept in play and I would have got to it, except a foot came out from over the touchline (the ref was at the other end) and over I went, to a chorus of 'Wanker!'

That match I was called every term of abuse that could possibly be in the dictionary, and a dozen other local ones such as 'sackless' and claht-head' – to say nothing of the ego-shattering directness of 'You're shit, player!'

That was all about embarrassment, and there's plenty of that in the game. You notice that most clearly when there are freak scores. One time, we played a team who only had nine men turn up. What should you do if you are an outfit of perfect gentlemen? Clearly, you should suggest that the game is re-arranged and then meet again with two full teams. What did we do? We played, and beat them 11 -2. Being our unhappy lot, there was an inquest on how and why two goals were scored against us by a team of nine men. Once again, it was excuses time. Someone said, 'A woman distracted me!' Another whine was 'I thought he'd blown for a foul!'

In Leeds we had freak scores which were reminiscent of those Australian Pools results, when you had figures such as Wamboromee 32, Chimwaromee 21.

There were a few 10-5's and 12-1's and in one game, when we punched above our weight, we lost 10-1 and they scored their first goal from the half-way line while our goalie was putting out his fag-end.

Strictly Not Ballroom

In between kicking a football in sixties Leeds, I was busy learning about pubs. Once, my drinking mate and I had drifted into this pub somewhere in the middle of the Gipton estate. It was packed, with very large people rammed shoulder to shoulder and smoke seeping into clothes and lungs, making eyes itch and throats sore. There was a line of folk at the bar and more behind them, raising howls or trying cajole or flirt with the barmaid.

We had sunk a few pints of bitter so the world was a happy place, but Dave and I had no idea how much more pleasure was to come.

It was the summer of 1966 and World Cup fever had spread like dazzling low winter sun across the human landscape, and I remember thinking that there was a good feeling in the air. Then, in seconds the crowd parted like the Red Sea and a voice called out, 'Now then, Jimmy's dancing!'

The sight was like watching a midget in a land of giants. The little man, dapper in a smart suit and trilby hat, with a crease in his trousers like a knife blade, danced with joy. It was like I'd seen in the old vaudeville acts at the Leeds Empire, something reminiscent of tap but without the metal-tipped shoes.

He smiled so that his face creased in a gurney smile, and the crowd clapped and whooped with him, not in derision at all. On he went, sometimes armed going akimbo and then on into a swinging rhythm. Someone asked, to the room in general, if the old bloke had won the football pools?

'He doesn't need a reason to dance, not old Jim!' came a reply from the smoke cloud.

Jim was maybe 70 but could have been anything between 50 and 80. Back in the sixties there was a lot of early ageing, maybe down to self-neglect and lack of everyday care. Hard graft had ground a lot down before retirement.

So Dave and I sat down and waited for Jim to stop, so we could try to get a drink. He did, but after what seemed like an hour but was really about three minutes. He took a bow and a voice from the depths told the landlord to give the man a pint.

Then there was my good self, in complete contrast. If ever there was a body made for watching dancing rather than trying to dance, it was mine. But this day I'd been on a bus back home from town when the smog came in like a dense yellowy breath from some giant who delighted in bringing the whole place to a stop. I felt my heart pound, thudding into my throat. When I did walk home I determined to have a skinful of ale that night, such had been the gunk stealing into my body. I felt like swilling out the pipes, as my Dad would have said.

It was a pub-crawl in the end, of safari proportions – one of the expeditions into parts of Leeds normally beyond the pale. One red-brick pub after another was visited, beer gulped, and then another place arrived on the increasingly blurred horizon, and its wares were sampled with determination rather than pleasure.

Then I came to a pub off the York Road, near the bus terminus, and it was vibrant with the kind of elation you only felt when reality had been thoroughly erased. I staggered into the dark and then moved through into the place; there were lights and flailing arms of women in disco heaven. I can recall only a few details, but basically the floor cleared so that the drunk could provide some entertainment. Maybe I was transmuted from drunk to Lord of Misrule.

It all ended in a long, sweaty walk home after missing the last bus. Pubs? You can keep 'em. That was the philosophical conclusion on the morning after.

In the steel town, you began to notice a similar thing. Women with a bit less to spend on clothes and make-up tend to settle for the second-best; men make for military or outdoors stuff, and you started to see more and more men ambling around Scunthorpe like Country & Western singers or Territorials with a dash of Woolworth's best yellow socks. The notion of looking good and feeling good gradually receded. They made do with whatever there was. Self-respect was part of what slipped away. But there was plenty of work being done to get it back.

Officials

With this is mind, what better, smarter and more powerful-seeming man could you have than the referee? He had to look like a man who knew the rulebook by heart, have a strong voice and a will to command equal to that of Monty in the desert. The refs had a verbal battle in every match we ever played in, as the poor devils usually had no trained linesmen to help them. Hence all decisions were challenged. But in that elegant black, the colour of Fascism, he was lord of all he surveyed and the whistle was his weapon. Those he disliked had the whistle blown just inches behind their ears.

Every game we had, we all knew that the ref would remember who had been the thorn in his flesh in the last debacle. He usually had a warmly ironical smile when he said something like, 'Now Smithy, I know you... and I don't want none of that Grand Opera... I'm not an opera buff and never will be, lad...'

In the midst of the cut and thrust of the game, the ref would have to be everywhere, with eyes in all directions. Different players would try to build alliances or corrupt them. You could always hear someone saying, quietly but firmly, 'Watch that number seven, John... he's a nasty piece of shit... broke a player's leg last year...' Or there would be the threats. 'You send him off and I'll come looking for you, Barry...What? You're sending me off as well? You can't do that.....'

We had one player in Leeds (called Nev) who upset every ref in the league. The reason being that he thought he knew more about the rules than anyone, including John Motson and maybe even the Wolstoneholme himself. On several occasions, this player would nag and tease the ref, throwing sarcastic lines such as 'Can you actually read, then ref?' or 'Were you born a tosser or have you studied it?' The player would wait until a notably bad decision and then just walk off, saying, 'I've had enough of this... can't play with this amateur...' The fact that we were down to ten men was no problem to him.

I spoke to one ref once who had worked in a minor league in Yorkshire. He said that a team manager had once threatened to have him 'seen to' after the game if the home team lost. When a leg was fractured in a tackle and the offender sent off, the manager ran on and whispered the threat again. In another match, he had to ask for protection from some of the players he knew, as he was punched walking off the field. I asked him if he did it for the love of the game. But no, he didn't love the game. He preferred cricket. Why did he go through the ordeal then?

'The dosh, mate... small as it is... but it buys me a holiday in Torquay...'

Medical expertise: a Case Study

Once or twice I played in goal. On the first occasion I foolishly stopped a piledriver with my hands in a very amateurish position and I felt a finger make a cracking noise. I was then in pain, and as more and more players came to look, I realised for the first time the limitations in the skills and qualifications of the imaginary supporting folk behind the team. Several men made macho comments like, 'dislocated ... pop it back in ...' but no-one dared actually do it.

After several minutes of consultation, I was driven to the casualty department and spent three hours waiting for a doctor to look at it. She snapped it back into place and I pretended to be tough.

But the sheer bumbling amateurism of the event had stunned me. I mean, supposing, like that poor French player who was walloped by the German goalie, I had swallowed my tongue and was choking to death. Would man after man have looked at me, shrugged, and said, 'Needs pulling back up ...' I had visions of some burly blokes with stubby fingers grappling with my tongue deep down in the windpipe and suffocating me.

Medical facilities? Zilch. Amateur medics? No way. It was that spray and the oranges, maybe a sponge, that's your lot.

Other minor injuries have included swollen foot, sore crotch, blurred vision, distended coccyx, pelvic throbbing, loose knee, crackling jaw, green big toe and goalie's elbow. The treatment?

Elastoplast and bitter beer. There was once talk, over a beer, of a proper first aid box. Regarding the contents of this, the strongest argument was for 'concentrate of Tetley's bitter, in little cubes. The other line of thought was that a nubile young woman should be employed as trainer's mate, to administer the new medicaments. In more recent times, when something called Sports Science was created, we could have had a student on work experience and therefore at no cost. That would have taken us beyond the Elastoplast and into the realms of abs and pecs (neither of which I ever had.)

Revie's Leeds Heroes 6

Terry Yorath

Readers might be expecting me to write about the big names; well, there are whole libraries on them, but Terry deserves a very honourable mention. It's time to celebrate the twelfth man.

In the years before Revie, when I first watched the matches, the team appeared to specialise in bizarre names such as Wilbur Cush and Grenville Hare. Yorath was not such a strange name, but it was memorable. When I was fresh from school and working out at Seacroft, my mate's sister claimed to be going out with Terry. He has been a familiar figure to me in more recent years, as my son began the traitorous behaviour of supporting Huddersfield Town and I had to drive him to home games and tolerate the Yorkshire enemies. Terry was there for some years as coach of course, and we met him when he signed his book. He was still the quiet man, steady and dependable, with firm opinions and good humour.

In the championship year he was emerging from what one commentator called 'perpetual reserve' to a player in his own right. It's true that he was called up to cover when injuries struck, but when interviewed at that time he was asked about life with the number 12 shirt and said, 'That makes it a better life. I think that you will find that Mick Bates and myself have played far better than when we have been in the first team... There are a lot of top clubs in the country, but Leeds United are something else again.'

He started for Leeds in a game against Burnley, when he was only 17, and then became a regular in the squad. He had the frustrating experience of being the sub in the 1973 Cup Final, in which Leeds lost 1-0 to Sunderland and later was in the team facing AC Milan in the UEFA Cup Final (1973) which again ended in defeat. In his nine years at Leeds he appeared 141 times and scored ten goals. But glory came when he was part of the team in 1973-4 when Leeds won the championship.

It has been said that the crowd got on his back, expecting him to be on a par with Bremner and Reaney, but to be fair, on many occasions that would have been when he was young, and standing in; people often expect the sub to be nothing more than a replica for the player they are covering.

Later he was a manager, at Bradford, and then he took charge of the Welsh team, and also later the Lebanon national team. He was a highly respected coach, both at Huddersfield and Bradford. If I had to sum up my memories and impressions, it would be that he had true grit, a sense of anticipation and could 'read' a game very smartly. You could see his skills in some of the Huddersfield mid-fielders in his time there, notably in Jonathan Worthington, for instance. Yes, in the end, his unusual name was easy to get right and he was easy to like when he turned out in that glorious white strip, when Leeds were like Real Madrid.

The place was in a trance, then, in 1983. But I was learning more about the boom years as I taught the workers on site. The foreign language class were coming on well, apart from the little Yemeni man who repeated the sounds of the alphabet every week and then forgot them by the end of the lesson. I told the students something about the men involved in making Scunthorpe so powerful in steel in years gone by. Men like Albert Jackson, who designed a new process of oxygen-blown steel making in 1958 and quickened up the whole business. But as usual, this led to a talk about work and speed and time: that was their favourite topic.

'Mr Steve ... everything is quick, quick yes? Why is this? In India it is slow, slow ... we are hot ...'

'Mr Steve ... why always you look at the clock on the wall?'

'Well, I have to finish the lesson at a certain time.'

'Mr. Steve ... that clock ... it is 20 minutes slow.'

One day someone asked me what steel was used for. I was amazed. Some men mumbled things like 'Cars.' And 'Buildings.'

But little Mr Carapino pressed his question. 'Do they make steel to last for always?'

Reading this, you probably guessed where that led. By three o'clock the man at the back who was a holy man had led us into philosophy again. They could all talk like Tom Paulin but English grammar and spelling was going to remain a mystery.

'Steve, mi amigo ... when you go to Espain, come and see my family.'

'Spain ... Spain ...'

'Si ... Espain. Espain ...'

The strangest dialogue I ever had in this class was about sex with the young. The intellectual from somewhere south of Yemen told me all about a book he had read about young people in the Middle Ages marrying when they were children.

"I thought this was puzzled upon, Mr Steve?"

"Frown ... frowned upon, you mean."

"Stop bloody correcting me and answer the question."

"Well, yes, in days gone by we did ..."

"But now you lock up the paediatricians I read. My brother is a paediatrician. He must take care."

I didn't correct him.

Every day, after the class on the works, I would see the hordes of men on bikes surging back out into the local freedom again after the bizarre world of steam, metal and greyness, all beneath that spouting, sulking spume of orange and brown from the massive sleeping giant of Appleby Frodingham. The finer points of the English verb tenses didn't matter much to that did it? I'd take the philosophy, and they had no interest in football.

But the humour in the class was always rich and rewarding, helping us work well, and take away some of the strain of knowing that the class was there because of trade union and management worries over health and safety.

'Mr Steve ... Pakistani men ... crap at soccer.'

I asked why. 'Where were the top players in the English league who were Asian?'

'This is simple question ... minding the shop ...'

He was called Kim by his mates; he was solid and clearly loved his food, and he told me that young Asian guys were very skilful with boxes, as he had seen them playing ball control with boxes of tea-bags and such.

Possibilities for the square-ball game? I think not, I told him. He didn't smile, and didn't see the joke. I think the square-ball game has a future, and should be placed in the Olympics, with Billy Connolly as the referee.

The foreign language class was progressing well. I made the mistake of mentioning Shakespeare one time, and they all wanted to know more.

"I heard about the guy", said the smart one at the back, who usually simply read his dictionary and smiled.

"Yes, he's famous," I said.

"Yes but is he any good? I mean, has he made big money?"

"Oh yeah, he did all right."

"All right? Did he have a sports car – a Maserati?"

"No," I smiled at that.

"Well he was a failure then. My brother has a Maserati and he's only written three poems."

I was stumped for an answer so they all chuckled, and I joined in.

8

We Won the Cup

How many men must have that fading photograph on the wall? Or the trophy on a shelf somewhere, or even in a drawer out of sight. This is the shield or trophy won with the heart and commitment of this Sunday league slog, foolishly risking life and limb for the team. It is surely a paradox that these significant awards in a man's life are generally an embarrassment, whereas at the time they were central to life. Maybe the answer lies deep in the British male psyche – the sense that a man was put on earth for combat and all that's left is Make the Deal in Two Minutes and the increasingly cultural shock of McScunthorpe or McWigan around the place.

It could be simply a part of an initiation rite. Once we were sent up into the mountains to slay our first creature and communicate with Manitou; now we win a trophy. Mine is a mahogany shield with a golden starburst and the words, Barton Regional Football League, and then those words that prompted a very long party one day: President's Shield Winner, 1983-4. Why this matters to me is that I was what was known in Churwell as a grec (runt) – the kid with no personality except being someone who collects stamps and never has any kit. I was the kid who, like Rain Man, collected cigarette cards or cards from Brooke Bond tea and swapped them endlessly, memorising daft facts. Once, I even collected some cards in packets of chewing gum with facts about foreign countries on them. For a few pence you could learn the Russian for 'so long' (Da svedanya it said) and that Moscow was the capital city.

So this geek finally proved he could do what his dad and his uncles did. Kick a ball straight or clear a cross out of the box. How could that ever happen? Somehow it did, and the team photo, in the moment of victory at the Brigg Town ground, almost makes us look like actual players. There are 14 of us, all in shirts of the same design (a huge step forward in professionalism) and two men, reserves on the day, wear suitably sporty looking jackets almost fit to run up and down the line in, like they do on *Match of the Day*.

Of course, the match itself is a blur. All you remember from games is about six events. This final had these:

Phase one. Shaky. Clear the bloody ball

Phase two. Shit. It's still no score, and this is Broughton

Phase three. Ye Gods, we scored

Phase four Shit. We gave a way a penalty

Phase five. Scuttling shuttlecocks ... we scored

Phase six. Shit. We won.

The men on the photo have the shield on the ground in front of them and they look mighty happy. The only worry for me is that I'm the only one not smiling. Why? It's that Leeds Puritanism again. That's why they always end up in bother – because they create it.

The cup-winning team 1983-4. I'm second from the left, back row, with the Hitler moustache, not looking like a winner at all, and suffering from a sore shin. The star was striker, Tony St Clair, sitting above the shield

The underdogs won of course. We were expected to be thrashed because the opposition were considered invincible. But it's amazing what you do on the day when the test comes. I even headed back to the keeper once – something that fills me with terror even today when Sol Campbell does it. Somehow, our goal poacher did it for us and everyone else just battled to stop the other side doing what they usually did. The celebration was loud and long, and for us, Wembley has got nothing on Brigg Town's ground.

In class, the next buzz word was Access. At first, the concept was roughly equated with *Educating Rita*. It was now the done thing to bring anyone into further education who had missed out or dropped out (or even been thrown out) of school. Scunthorpe was ripe for this, and we had a boom on our hands again. We read that the town and indeed the whole industry across Britain was 're-structuring' and that people from their thirties to their fifties mostly were searching either for a second career or simply looking for themselves inside that person who had avoided or failed 'the system.'

The interviews were long and complicated. We were dealing with people who would be doing advanced study but yet were without paper qualifications. The town was teeming with men and women who had very specific skills, like running slag off a furnace or being a pig-carrier (removing pig iron from the beds) but these were hardly transferable. In fact, no-one used the word transferable because in the past one skill had been enough.

Access courses gave new skills but also opened up the 'Humanities' debate again. The whole conflict of useful and useless knowledge was built into the studies. The magical world of Culture was suddenly offered for real to people (mostly women) who had been good wives or nine-to-fivers with marriage-supermarket-television at the core of their experience.

We ran courses on sociology, literature, history and

economics. Everything there was subversive. My colleagues and I would meet to talk about the restlessness in these good people, who were like defenders suddenly realising that sometimes you were allowed to run up field and have a shot at goal. When they did, the celebrations were orgasmic. Never in my teaching career have I seen so many huddles, supportive gestures, laments of disappointment and appeals for help in such basics of life as What to Read and What to Write.

Marriages and long-term relationships were rocked and wrecked by these questions. They wanted to know everything, not just about steel and iron and soaps and pubs. This is not being superior: it's just that drama and sonnets and the nature of being a gay writer were not just new, they were revolutionary. Around 90 percent of students were women in their thirties, and they were mixing anger with subversion. When my bum had been worth watching, they confessed that they made me write on the blackboard just to watch it. Now, they would prefer the blackboard.

A typical conflict was the theatre trip which lasted much longer than we expected. We had been to London, I think, for *Hamlet*. One female student was loving this whole business of ideas and thinking for yourself. But she was married to a businessman who was resenting her not being there at home with tea and cakes like a nice, dutiful housewife. We trundled into the college car park at about two in the morning, and in an age before mobile phones, it had been impossible to tell the man how late we would be.

He had been waiting in the car park for three hours. There was a yelling and a screaming enough to rival a core scene in a Stephen King movie. I think a few fundamentals were sorted out that night in two people's lives. He would have to start living and learn to love Shakespeare, or, finito.

One class was grappling with the history of the campaign of universal suffrage and the Chartists of the 1830s. When I explained about the military extremism of some of the radicals, there was universal approval. The general feeling was that to change the world you had to kick ass. This, from a score of people who had crept into the enrolment room just four months before, with self-esteem as low as the tide in Holland.

That evening had been like a film set, it was so extreme and dramatic. Some of the seething, restless demands for renewal went like this:

'I never did nothing at school and I'm sick of pratting about...'

'I just watch telly... there has to be more...'

'Now, my daughter, she's reading *Romeo and Juliet*, so I want to as well...'

'I'm actually 64 and... well, I hope you don't think it's too late because I'm going for it, and   I've already bought the books'

'Do you get a certificate ... and how soon can you have letters after your name?'

For me, the spirit of the town was manifested in one particular woman who had been caring for her elderly mother for most of her life, and the mum had died that summer, just two months before the woman sat in the hall and browsed through a hundred leaflets. I asked her what she wanted to do, and she was hesitant. Her face looked confused, but then, without a trace of a smile, she said, 'I need to do something that will sort of ... well ... make up for lost time ...'

What do you answer? I can't recall what I said. But she joined up and discovered a talent for music and photography. In fact, her creative soul had been walled up somewhere and had been screaming to get out with every bed she made, every cup of tea she took upstairs.

When you give a place something special, you take away its scope to be different. Brigg, up the road just eight miles away, is always Brigg Fair. Lincoln, 24 miles south, has the cathedral and the imp. These things are infinite. But steel tends to have a limit on who wants it and what can be done to use it in new ways. If you lose that, you have either nostalgia or the heritage industry, and while you cultivate these things, the people still have to make a living.

So where do old footballers go when their one thing is done? My Dad had to stop when he injured his arm. He joked to the doctor that he wasn't playing cricket. But he stopped anyway. I never saw a trophy that he might have won, but he had the autographs. He'd seen and met some greats, like Wilfred Mannion and Ted Drake.

The mid- to late-Eighties with their Access and their restructuring meant that everything in the media was telling you to be different, to reinvent yourself. I noticed that it was becoming tougher to resist change when the Yuppie philosophy was encroaching, and there was a defiant rearguard action against slickness on the pitch as in life. The cup-winning side moved into a low gear again and seemed happier with the game, rather than the result.

You know something is on the turn when you go small-scale: I began to fancy five-a-side and went jogging. The team mattered less and less. I'm sure it was something related to a deep desire to be a loner, an individual. Teams were not so appealing any more.

That's what Access and Late Developers are all about: they shout, 'Let me be me... you never did!'

The most telling moment came one day when I was discussing Larkin's *Church Going* with a class. We split beautifully down the middle – those who wanted to judge Larkin himself, mostly as 'a miserable old man' and those who loved the poem's statement of uncertainty of the appeal of the mystery, of place and permanence. I could see that society was dividing.

This was the restlessness:

The Housewife's Tale

I went to the class to stretch myself.
That's what they say: stop the glazed stare
Grabbing me as it does in Asda.

This lecturer asked me about Emily Bronte.
What I thought of her imagery.
Well, I said it made me shiver,
Gave me bad dreams. A cold book, I said.
He seemed to like that and I expected a tick:
A long red tick on the paper, like the kids get.

When it came on the telly, the film, I mean,
I couldn't keep my mouth shut. Something
Burst in me like a bike tyre. It was garbage.

Ron told me to shut up so I knitted.
Every bloody jumper I've made is wool and hate.
A new blend. Emily made them, though,
You bet she did – and shivered in them.

9

Hanging up the Boots

Defeat rubs shoulders with triumph. A community down on its knees learns to run or disappear. In football terms it's the ten-man team paradox. The team down to ten men often plays better. I think people in the steel town knew that in the eighties. Football wraps up this community grit somehow and takes care that it survives.

I went to a match at the Old Show Ground not long before Scunthorpe United closed it down and moved to the new Glanford Park. I had every thought about community confirmed there, just as I did at Boothferry Park when I went to watch Hull City play Scarborough, and at a time when both were low down. It was something underneath the robotic chants and it's in the humour too. On the terraces in Hull, one group were singing 'I'm City till I Die' and within minutes, a lone voice with a 'posh' southern accent shouted, very tamely, 'Come on City!' It was as if some Tory Lord had been there rather than in a box at Chelsea. Everyone laughed.

At the Old Show Ground, even the man who always bellowed out 'Sack Barlow' was quiet that day. The clichés all seem to apply: pull together ... get your ducks in a row ... together we are strong. There are photographs of the marches during the 1981 strike, and there is the same mood, existing somewhere between desperation and love: the banners say, 'Can this town afford the end of an era of steel-making?' and 'Workers don't hide ... We will march ... we still have our pride.' The faces are dour; the mood solemn, and the marchers are well wrapped up against the typically cold weather. But everything in the image suggests a community, a need.

My student, Graham Randall, when he wrote his essay about the last day at Normanby Park, was rightly in an elegiac mood; but in another sense there is always that nagging feeling that the end of an era opens up surprises. My Access students sensed this; but leaving the pitch was another matter. The lad inside you protests; the idea that there is no more 'play' is a raw deal. My life had had its cyclical movements in this respect, my football days suspended when I went to study in Wales, but I always knew that I would put the boots on again.

I think of my Dad, what he must have felt when the doctor told him to stop playing. You can imagine all the words of advice from wife and mother, brother and father: 'Don't take any risks, lad ... that arm o' thine ... it might be crocked for life if tha plays again ...' I can feel his churning up inside. The game was so deeply settled in him, like something nesting in the spirit. Not to trot out onto his Tanhouse pitch again ... beyond belief. Even the war didn't take that pitch away – it was there waiting for him when he came back.

I can't imagine his last game. After all, it's a game in which words matter but in the end you can play without saying a word, just lose yourself in the total involvement. What was he going to involve himself in then, in 1955? Selling groceries? What a drop down, from stoking in minesweepers and going up for headers in a rain storm ... God, lacing up his boots for the last time must have been a little death, a farewell worth a poem, not a grunt and a slap on the back. Here was a young man who had been directed in every move in his life so far: to school, to war, to shop-work. Now it was going to be no more adventures, he must have thought.

How does a community hang up its boots? Do places die slowly? It's a case of sloughing of skins. The typical young married man of the early eighties would have a profile involving a young wife with some dreams to forget; luxuries out of the question, and hope in something else he could be, later, when he had become another version of what they both had known and accepted.

On a larger scale, Scunthorpe, like most places, has been part of that massive seduction, replacing the hand-skills a man has to have with gaudy clothes, management-speak and fast-food jobs. My Dad was maybe no different, travelling around Leeds in a Co-op van, no different from a young man in corporate red and green serving at a Scunthorpe drive-thru. That could bring thoughts down as low as an ant's belly. But something English wins through, and a lot of that is seen on that green rectangle on a Sunday morning.

This has been my tribute to a place, some people and the beautiful game. Looking at a chunk of social history through football somehow supplies a torch in the darkness. It goes on, this obsession, relentlessly, and no-one knows how, when or why a young person identifies with that great game. My son, at the age of eight, liked Manchester United colours and players (most boys do, unfortunately); but now, as a young man, he inexplicably supports a sinking, cash-strapped team called Huddersfield Town. He even jokes and calls them Huddersfield Mediocre.

I have stood on the terraces at the McAlpine Stadium and the KC Stadium with him, and the feeling has been the same: a deep sense of sharing something as mysterious as the stars and the Milky Way. Some call it a tribe. I've even been called, when I was playing, 'one of those degenerates who kick each other once a week.' But all this is meat and drink to me.

A few months ago I walked with my son from a car park at the top end of Huddersfield, through town, following the same streets that he does as a ritual. We walked past every stereotype you could imagine, just as in J B Priestley's seminal essay on football, *T'Match*, when he talks of 'Bruddersford'. You walk past a gasworks, with a Working Men's Club beneath it, and then you cross a river and a canal.

On that canal, with bushes bent down dipping into the brown waters and discarded push-chairs and bikes projected from it, there lives a kingfisher. I have seen him dipping and diving; I never told my son this, but that bird is for me an image of that optimism football brings with it as part of the package. This is a bright hope in the grimy mills and grey streets. Is there any wonder that we spend £50 on a new strip? It's colour, it's optimism and it's showing that you can be a kingfisher, not a rusting bike.

The Churwell Connection

The last part of this story is completed by a revisiting of my Dad's world at Churwell WMC, my debut season as a Sunday league player, and the final ironical Scunthorpe connection.

It begins with a slice of boy's world in the Leeds suburbs around 1956. This was when I was still in the Hopeless case and Gormless category at school and did anything to avoid physical exercise.

As I sit writing this in the steel town, Allan Clarke is living just over a mile away from me. He now earns his money selling ventilation systems. We know nothing of each other, yet as a boy I would watch him from the Elland Road terraces. In a passing conversation with a local man, I've been told that Paul Madeley, the workhorse utility player for Revie, has had a heart by-pass operation. There is a tough irony in this, as it reminds us all, the football die-hards, that fame is short-lived and that only in the memories of the true terrace-dweller will the really special players live on.

But we do have something that for me started in 1956 at that time when I was hooked on trivia and indoor stuff. We have the magic of the football fact-book. In these solid old (often red-covered) reference works of the middle years of the twentieth century, we have our biggest clue about where the mania begins. My mania for this started with something far more ephemeral.

It was a fusion of two things happening around that time: my family may have had no time for book buying, but we were drowning in weekly and monthly comics. *The Wizard* and *The Rover* became the imaginative centre of my boy-world, winning me over where school had dismally failed. One day, as the comics tumbled through the letter box, I noticed that one had a free gift: a strip of black and white photographs of hands-folded football stars looking dourly at me. You didn't need colour to feel the power of a Sheffield Wednesday shirt or a sleeves-rolled-up, no-nonsense defender's glare from such as Wilfred Mannion.

This gave me the collector's itch. From that day I set out to scuff, bend and smear the cards as they were held in my grasp, available for swapping on the street.

At the same time I became aware that my Dad's career as inside-left was under threat. In a particularly heated local derby he was led off in pain. I was stunned that it was his arm, not a leg, that was giving him the agony. Looking back, I wonder if he was prone to elbowing and being elbowed. But that seems to be ungentlemanly. Then, you could bundle Bert Trautman into the netting and crack his neck, but it was considered unseemly to set about an outfield player with your arms. Kicking was fine; the odd clattering tackle, knees, tibs and fibs open to splits and cracks, was accepted. But I'm not sure about elbows. I envisage my Dad perfecting a rotor-blade ascent for the high cross, mastering the occult art of hovering by the side of the opponent, arms merely flapping at the wrist.

Dad had this dodgy arm. It wouldn't move when you wanted it to. In Churwell around 1955 you didn't bother with doctors unless you turned blue or the genitals turned to plasticine. But this case moved from puzzling to annoying to quite bad. It ended in a trip to Leeds Infirmary.

So here was my Dad with an arm problem that made him give up football. Well, we were about to move across the city to a northern suburb and he was having to pack in the game anyway. The photograph of his team was proudly placed on the mantelpiece by the tub of spills and a bowl of farthings.

It didn't seem long before my Uncle Harry's van arrived (the one used normally to carry pigs) and we were moved to Halton. There I began the card collection and the hoarding of football comics, then record books and annuals. That last word gives me a thrill, of pleasure as I write it. The Christmas Annual was the embodiment of all the poetry and ritual involved in the Beautiful Game. Just to see that shiny patina of gaudy colour on the cover, and the centre-forward nutting the ball in, was enough to give a frisson of inexplicable joy.

It was in the annuals that I learned about the games with amazing score lines, like the unthinkable 4-6 result, or the fact that some men had scored as many as six hat-tricks. Then there were the old photos: images of goalies who would by today's standards be considered recruits for club doorman careers but never for a life between the posts.

But there were always the stories of the team. They became legendary. Like the tale of the trainer who was a grease monkey, and gave a player on the touchline, in pain and suffering, the cold water treatment, the mucky flannel instead of the clean one. The man played the rest of the game looking like a stray from *The Black and White Minstrel Show*, and didn't know why the others were laughing at him. The trainer was scared of change and innovation: discussion of the addition of a plaster to the First Aid box disturbed him.

The Debut Again

Of course it had to happen one day: long after school in my teens, the debut game for Rose Forgrove in the Sunday league. There was a crowd around Dad, but he did walk across to watch me by myself at one point. By debut I mean, the one he came to watch. He was puzzled about why I had never been interested in playing at school, but now I was keen. I had bought the Woolies' boots, padded up and trotted out to play on the left wing. I knew he was coming to watch but he wasn't there at the kick-off, so I spent most of the first half glancing round looking for him. Then, a high ball came down towards me and I instinctively knew that I would have to trap it. If I didn't trap it, then it would slap me in the groin and then bounce into touch. My right foot went up and I fixed my stare at the ball. It soared down to my, then only half-lodged under the boot, and spun out of play.

A voice behind said, "Good effort to trap, son." It was Dad, and that was all he said through the whole game. After, he said, "You did well. We'll get some Wall Game time in. That'll help."

So it was a case of more Wall Game, him and me feverishly running around the back yard heading and side-footing balls under the chalk line behind us. He would work up a sweat and turn bright red. But nothing could stop him. I began to see why he was one of the They Shall Not Pass breed and had been booked a few times.

The debut game was in a park off the Gipton estate, by the road to the Oakwood Hotel. I was amazed that there was a crowd. But the game then was such a different thing. Even the guys in the national celebrity bracket were not of such a status that they made park football a worthless spectacle, and little huddles of keen family groups would be on the line, drinking tea and laughing. They were noisy in this, my first full game. I was desperate to impress and I know that at one point I headed the ball in front of me and sprinted after it, only to hit what felt like a grazing elephant but turned out to be the goalie. He was a man with the dimensions of Robbie Coltrane but made of concrete. I had a headache all day.

Not long after came the first trips to Elland Road and I began to experience that link between the images in comics and the actual people. The first team I saw had names that became my first poetic litany. My poetics I owe to these men: Wilber Cush, Georgie Meek and Alan Peacock. The last name was my first idol. He was a triangular, wide-shouldered header of the ball with solidity and finesse. Then, the team were The Peacocks, not the Whites (how dull is that?) and his name was the name of the team, and also the name of two pubs close by, the Old and the New Peacock. That meant that for me, Alan WAS Leeds United. Until John Charles came along, naturally. But the point is that the faces you saw in comic line-drawings were now there, still distant, but real men.

I was in danger of becoming that oddball entity, the football dreamer-poet. I would scribble verses and mutter fast-paced commentaries on imagined games. These were pre-Subbuteo days of course, so blow-football was all I had at home. But there was nothing to stop a man doing a commentary as he walked to work. I had a two-bus trip to the Forgrove factory on Dewsbury Road, and this gave me time to learn my French vocabulary and then squeeze in some football poetry. The only lines I recall from these epic-writing days are:

> To Peacock then, and with a firm head to the net,
> The Wolves keeper makes a dive he will forget.
> And the crowd rise in one relentless din,
> Oh yeah, the big man's headed in....

The notebooks of this stuff have long gone, mostly spurned when I read T S Eliot and went all High Culture, only to return in later and wiser years to my roots. Now, the real poetry is in Bremner's statue and the Drysalter's; the Cottingley cemetery where the previous Wades lie at rest, and the words echoing still, "Fine play, that man...." And "Well in there, Cush."

If there are spirits in there, close to Gildersome's old valley, they are playing the Wall Game at midnight and talking about Peacock and Charles.

My notebook and ephemera are in a solid family tradition. My Dad's autograph book is the classic: faded now, it was once gold and classy; he has written the usual baloney such as 'If this book should chance to roam, smack its bum and send it home.' He also adds details of the school team and notes that he is down as inside right. This is the 'scool team' for 1938. The team plan is included in a book with the autograph of Len Hutton, a large picture of 'Thomas Holley' next to which is Dad's information: 'A Leeds United Half Back' and Holley's autograph. Other stars include Wilfred Mannion of Middlesbrough and Ronnie Clayton of Blackburn.

Dad's boots were hung up after that long-standing injury and a move away from Churwell. 'Hard but fair' sums him up. Strangely, looking at all the formal positions such as outside-right and half-back makes the game seem more distant than it really is. After all, changes have not been that extreme. For a fan, the most radical changes have been the divisional organisations. Long gone are the days when the television results would cover 'Third Division' or 'Fourth Division South.'

Hanging up the boots, just to be sentimental for a moment, is one of the saddest phrases in male vocabulary. The phrase stretches into a general metaphor as well. It suggests inactivity, the beginnings of that phase in life when the old man nods at the still mud-caked boots, desiccated and deformed, strung up by old sacks and bags, and says, 'I've long ago hung up me boots, son.' The only reaction is to laugh or else a poem might come on, and we wouldn't want that. Footballers don't, I'm still told, ever cry. Paul Gascoigne was to prove that very wrong.

10

Lust for Learning

I have in my memory three photographs, all from the 1950s. These tiny Brownie snaps say it all but at the same time say nothing: Grandma Schofield with her flowery summer frock rolled up so she could paddle, looking quizzically at the camera, her black hat still firmly pinned to her hair against the North Sea breeze. Then there is a real action shot: my Dad, arm out to take a catch in a game of beach cricket. He is just growing that paunch after too much Tetley's bitter and lardy breakfasts. Then finally, the family group squat on the golden sands: my mother in her long cotton dress and rather Nordic-looking blonde hair; me with spade, leaning against her while sitting on a heap of sand; and my Dad, heavy working trousers screwed up to resemble shorts, his young father's smile, as he sits bare to the waist, in his personal heaven.

My Dad's heaven was Filey on the East Yorkshire coast, and we would have a week or two in Filey every summer, usually staying in a caravan. All three photos are of Filey scenes. Not much else in the year was deemed suitable for a memorial image. The other days, weeks, months in 1952 were spent in hard toil, of course. Mam was bending over a sewing machine, on piece-work at a place in the centre of Leeds, right next to where the traffic now gathers before splitting into the vehicles bound for the M1 and those going to the M62.

Me at Filey around 1952. Even then I had no ball control, and I'm handling in the box

For Dad the week was spent behind a counter in the grocers', exuding charm; his professional white coat and the slight film of flour powdering his head made him seem a spirit of the place. If Filey was his heaven, then right next door were the conviviality of the pub or club and the bookie's office. He was a man of simple tastes, but the life needed a certain amount of income, and he was slipping into Micawberdom even from this early date.

The three images evoke much that was typical of life for the workers in fifties Leeds. Leisure was dominated by beer, jokes, football and talk about what was happening when time off came along. Everything else was just daily graft and had to be tolerated. As to Grandma Schofield, well, at this point she was in well-earned retirement, after a life of hardship in Beeston and Hunslet, areas of Leeds characterised by red-brick terraces and factories, inter-war poverty and large families. Florence Schofield was no exception: she had seven children and was, in 1952, beginning to have time for the grandchildren. This was her idea of heaven.

The passion for learning in late developers burned hot and long in the college of the steel town, and I had been arguably the template for the school failure who found learning as the great discovery of life, after leaving the classroom at 15 for the world of work. I knew that I had a special rapport with these new students, coming to college to look for something new, some possibility of productive change.

My own learning began with the love of books – well before I could read. Although useless at school as an infant, and terrified of English classes, nevertheless I collected books, mainly the red-covered classics made for new readers. I loved the shape and feel of them, the mere possession of them. It was as if they contained some magical properties of transmutation, like the fabled philosopher's stone. I was destined to double-rack old smelly tomes and spent much of my time searching for books at the back, stored in heaps.

Beneath that mute adoration of the written word by a boy who could only read a few pages of Janet and John, the school reading text, lay the future logophile and crazy autodidact, a young adult who was drunk on words. The real moment of epiphany, the experience that created the future teacher of adults, came in an evening class in Leeds when the 'A' level English course began.

Mr Smith used most of the first lesson doing something that no English teacher could possibly do now without his or her job being threatened: he read aloud the whole of D H Lawrence's long story, 'Odour of Chrysanthemums'. We were all entranced. Not for one moment did any of the 20 students appear to be restless or bored. I was totally enraptured by the rhythms of the prose and by the human community at the centre of the story.

Yes, I wanted to be Mr Smith. I wanted to send people home, after two hours in a dour classroom on a winter evening up north, with a burning love of literature in their souls. I started writing poetry: I read everything I could manage in the working day, in between calculating wages in an engineering factory office. I went to the theatre in Harrogate and in Leeds, and then bought and read the script of the play I had seen.

I have always kept notebooks, and that I owe to Mr Smith as well; he said a lot about cultivating the habit of being creative. This came down to succinct advice: don't wait for the Muse to call – ask her in. I've always remembered that. My notebooks are full of quotes, stories, jokes and snippets from interviews with writers. It makes a fascinating contrast to my Dad's book: mine is all wordy and his is all pictures. I think he really dreamed of being a professional footballer, but I wanted to be a writer like John Braine or David Storey, giving the world the real truth about the gritty world of the North. Most of all, my night-school experience prompted me to carry forth the great Gospel of Learning to the greater world out there. I'm writing that facetiously because, looking back to that time, I was quite a snob, full of myself. In fact, my lust for learning, in the 1970s when I was still a student – of Dialectology at Leeds – led me into something that taught me more about Churwell and about that interesting split in the working-class person who goes away to grab some education.

Just like D H Lawrence, I was the son of working-class parents and I went to train as a teacher, but before that I did my degrees, first in English and then the dialect study. In the latter I needed a project topic, and there it was right in front of me: Uncle Albert, quarry gaffer and dialect speaker. I decided to interview him.

It was an uneasy thing: I sat there with my little tape recorder and asked him what he said in certain situations. Most of the answers were not in dialect but in expletives, something like this:

'What did you call the wagon that you used?'

'A ****** little bastard.'

'Thanks. And what did you call this tool on this picture?'

'A ******* little ******* bugger.'

'Thanks Uncle Albert, but I can't use that.'

Still, it was all part of learning. Half of me, in the pubs at vacation time, found some words to chat about the team; the other half was always wanting to talk books. The result was that I made myself a den, a writer's garret, and I became the Leeds version of the Misunderstood Artist, alone and harbouring a profound message that the world must hear. I wrote poems that had very little to do with Leeds United, such as this masterpiece:

> 'I'm reaching for some shapeless thing.
> What it is I do not know.
> Where happiness reigns and people sing
> And the cheeks of children glow...'

The sad thing is that I didn't know how bad it was, but filled a notebook with this gush and then brooded, walking the dark streets, feeling like the artist damned to loneliness. But football kept on calling.

I eventually realised that you could actually write poems about real life, not about dreamy landscapes and pretty flowers. The result was that I bought my clothes at the Army and Navy Stores and started smoking. Yes, I would be the Working-Class Writer, a man with his hands mucky and a stain on his soul caused by a mix of nicotine and a rankling grudge against the capitalists – though I wasn't sure whether Mam was a capitalist or not, because she kept a shop in Leeds. I was, under all this, a crusader for words and poems.

That crusader for writing and imagination was me in the steel town much later: still the same questing mind with a desire to spread the good news about 'great writing.' Really, I had little power of discrimination – anything that was the written word was fine. It had to be devoured.

At the college, after the flood of adult students came and the town worked hard to redefine itself after the Normanby Park closures, the English teaching moved into degree territory. It was the time when universities created franchised degrees, so people in the catchment areas could apply to study for the first year of their degree (in foundation studies) at their local college, and so save the time and expense of travel at least for a year.

I became the course leader for a degree in Combined Studies and another in Humanities; that meant that I could teach the literature I wanted to teach, for the first time at a level matching my own studies. It was sheer joy. Students and I had some exciting debates and explanations, into the style and meaning of writing. There is nothing like having to explain fundamental concepts to beginners. Topics such as 'reader reception' for instance, all about how and why we read and what personal and social uses and outcomes reading has (and I never enjoyed this side of English teaching), were up for discussion. It was a brief, on my part, to point out how little innocence was left in reading stories in our complex and multicultural age.

To build on this, we had trips to talks and plays. A typical class might have a scholarly type who wanted to read everything; an extreme-right political type who had a way of engaging in love-my-own-voice discourse, and several students who had arrived at degree studies after by-passing traditional GCE channels. The efforts to expose the students to literary culture were not only strenuous but inventive and determined. One trip involved myself and three students travelling 60 miles in my little Ford Fiesta to meet the novelist Stan Barstow. His best advice was to focus on one thing and do it well: 'I only write books,' he said, with his lisp, 'don't bother with the fripperies and other stuff. Just concentrate on the books.'

My life settled down to a pattern of teaching, football and family life. My son was born in 1978 and so I had to reshuffle my sense of self to accommodate the notion of being a dad. That was very unsettling. Being a dad was a challenge in every sense. There was now another person in addition to self and wife: all kinds of changes happened, such as pushing him around in the pram at one in the morning, to try to give him sleep. By the time he was five or six and declared his love of the Manchester United strip, I found that the old enemy had crept into my life deviously: Leeds fans detest the name Manchester United, and that goes wide and deep – more than the equivalent of the cricket enmity in the Roses matches. The fact is that the Reds are so damned good, so infuriatingly successful, that it rankles for Leeds fans, deprived of glory since Revie – and that is ancient football history now.

One football match was a guest appearance for another local team – the police – who were short of defenders near the end of the season, and so in desperation they turned to me. It was very cold that day and there was frost on the pitch. Near the goalmouth there was another of those vicious curled-up fans of hard soil. There was a blade of tough earth like a knife and yes, as I went to stop a striker I went over and my face landed on this. The striker went on to score, so it had been a repeat of the one mentioned earlier. Once again, I took the blame. 'Your fault, player. You played him on side!'

The last time this happened I had had to give a talk the day after. This time it was an exam board. For the first ten minutes of the meeting various lecturers asked if it had been a good stag night or 'What happened to the other guy?' Again, the only way to shut them up was to say, 'Pardon my appearance but I've been...'

'Yes, you've been playing football again,' someone said.

The question of the strip came up again. It had always been vaguely blue but now we finally regulated this so that there were eventually eleven men on the pitch with the same dark and light blue-striped strip. Naturally, this had to be paid for, so the request for payment was made in the changing-room (as we never met at any other time) and grudgingly, everyone paid up. Obviously, there was no second strip, so if we had a clash of colours, it was back to the Harlequin outfit of many colours. But in one match we did play another team who had a blue strip a bit like ours. Why we did this I will never know. The opposition had a natty strip with the single blue stripe down the white shirt, like Crystal Palace used to have; the game was a farce, with cries of 'He's one of them!' every few minutes. A ball might be passed to a blue blur out on the wing, only for the man in question to hear cries of anger or chuckles of amusement as the opposition took the ball and went forward. This affair was only a close second-best in the chronicle of farces we had – second only to the game in the fog. So desperate were we to play that we played in a thick mist, and that lasted for three minutes when the ref decided that 'This is madness!'

A cool, impressive strip means a lot in terms of the psychology of the game, but in the end this does not guarantee success. I've seen one team, an outfit who jogged out onto the pitch acting like Real Madrid about to play West Snitterfield WMC, actually play like a set of dummies in an arcade game, standing still and swinging a leg now and again. Our raggle-taggle bunch of scruffs beat them easily – a very rare event in our history.

At college, the cultural trips went on, and matters hit an all-time low when we had a trip to see *King Lear* at the Liverpool Everyman. My 30 students and their friends were excited at the prospect and arrived in good time, quiet and well-behaved, with their coffee-flasks and newspapers ready for the journey. What we didn't know was that the previous week a music club went to a gig in this company's coach and left the interior looking like the scene after a clash between Hell's Angels and American Outlaws.

An old mobile scratching shed arrived to take us to Liverpool: it was not the smart, streamlined affair we expected, being cultural and nice; I didn't realise it at the time, but there was trouble brewing. We had been given an old crate that was about to explode or disintegrate – the company couldn't care which.

Somewhere in the middle of wild Lancashire on the M62 smoke began to appear from under the boards of the coach floor. The driver pulled over and we were all evacuated. After an hour of standing and waiting for help that was never going to come, I begged the driver to try to move the thing, and we did move, everyone piling back in. We were 20 minutes late and I was so stressed that I spent the interval in a pub to recover. I spent most of the journey home praying that there would be no more smoke, and I had to pretend that I had seen the production. But if there is one skill in which English teachers excel it is in talking knowledgeably about books and plays they have never read or seen.

The determination of mature students to get an education is incredibly impressive and often very moving to watch. This is most evident in those who have an illness or a serious handicap. The blind or visually impaired students I have known illustrate this admirably. They show a will to have knowledge, and with exceptional determination. But there is a humorous side, and this is when guide dogs appear. The first I recall is a beautiful black Labrador called Benny, who would sit under a desk and indulge in very loud sighs and moans. I'm sure he calculated exactly the most powerful and poignant moments of the class in which to inject his most excruciating moan of tedium. The result was my heightened explanation of a line of Keats, for instance, something like this: 'Keats, knowing he was near death, and coughing blood into his handkerchief, reflected on the transience of life (loud and prolonged canine whine, as the creature is suffering on the rack of literary boredom) then pause for the laughter of the class. Then I tended to say, ' And as Benny knows only too well, life can be torture, particularly when a dog has to listen to teachers droning on about John Keats.' I think that Benny registered the word 'Keats' and he always thought Keats were tasty morsels likely to appear in the middle of dull English classes to appease him.

Then there was Maureen, a student who will always symbolise for me the sheer will to win, to achieve. She came to three of my module courses and in each one her sight was progressively deteriorating. At first it was a desperate rush to read, to devour print while she could still manage reading novels. Then the support and the gadgets arrived to help, and technology with its full armoury. Finally the dog joined her, another floor-level student who had no interest at all in literary theory.

Maureen had missed school and had discovered books and learning, and like Willy Russell's Rita, 'wanted to know everything' That is a noble aim, something I have often found in adult education classes. For many students in that context, the lust for learning is unstoppable, as if some huge lake beneath the surface was at last gurgling up into the light. Selection and sifting is then the hard part for the teacher: how to help sort out the reliable knowledge from the suspect – and what is 'truth' anyway?

In the team, the period after winning the cup was an anti-climax. The form and dash of every team goes through peaks and troughs. We were thoroughly in a trough. For some of us the ageing process brought dodgy joints and limited mobility. The left-back began to be dazzled and tricked by the younger strikers; the mid-field seemed to enjoy ball-watching. Nobody dare mention 'training' in any place except the pub, and then the word was spoken with a smile and brought a snigger in response.

But then we discovered five-a-side. This is the version of football reserved for psychopaths who have slowed down.

In this mini-pitch torture chamber with tiny goals and an assortment of confusing red and yellow line-markings, the objective is to try to score goals by swift teamwork, deft dribbling and delicate chips or banana shots. In truth, the arena becomes a place where the solid, rather slow guys collect the ball and then blast a shot at the keeper with all the pent-up aggression of a day at the hellish office behind it. I have suffered several dislocated fingers, injured ankles and deep purple bruises in 'friendly' matches. Also, there is never a referee in this version of the beautiful game, so disputes can be a touch loud and violent. Blokes may walk off in a huff, vowing never to play again with 'you bloody tossers.' The argument they have is really with themselves, and they don't see that having a crowd witness this sad scene is making everything much worse.

Tackles and shoulder-charges often result in players limping off, throwing expletives to the world in general and the most outrageous assaults are laughed off in a false spirit of manly laissez-faire. Although there was one player who tended to pick up the ball and sulk if a really hard shot was fired. One time, after a shot so vicious that the goalie had moved out of the way to save his life, this player ran for the ball, picked it up and said, 'So this is what we call football then is it?' He went on to explain the nature of five-a-side and how the previous year he had suffered concussion in one of our matches. His tirade brought a few minutes silence and then someone said, 'Give us our ball back please!' He went home in a bad mood.

On one occasion he ranted for ten minutes, giving a speech something like: 'So we're going to forget all about football are we – we're going to play Nazi style are we? Is that the idea? Why don't we all just get a black strip with military arm-bands and play Hitler's rules? And whoever said that you, Trevor, played like an ageing Geoff Hurst? I'd say you were more like Al Capone with a grudge!'

But incredibly, five of the team entered a five-a-side competition, and won the cup – without any rough stuff or strong-arm tactics. Baby-Faced Nelson strategies were left out and the team persisted in the league after that, confidence boosted. We specialised in what might be called stylish mediocrity mixed with working-class grand opera every Sunday morning.

A Special Medical Note on the Ball-Crusher

The subject of team banter needs a further look. It exists as a form of torment that is like no other and it stems from the player's belief that he is made of iron when in fact he is made of something close to cardboard. You have a 'knock' – meaning anything from a broken shin to a black eye, and that invites teasing – but there is nothing like the ball in the er.... groin.

The location in question lies neatly inside the tunica vaginalis and scrotal sack; curled around it (the testis) is the epididimys and the pampiniform plexus. The ductus deferens also lies close by. This is all good stuff for the medical student, but what it means on the pitch is that the ballocks, despite all these coverings, are subject to being battered by a football and the result is agony. The result – teasing.

The ball-crusher shot or clearance tends to flatten the receiving player and there is general laughter and shouts of phrases usually with the phrase 'family prospects' or similar. This is the ultimate test of the Sunday player. If he carries on, taking the flak, then the immortal words of Kipling come to come.. 'You'll be a man my son.' You may never have children, but never mind. A grimace is permitted. A yelp of pain is considered acceptable. But anything related to Grand Opera is frowned upon.

11

The Joys of Failure

As a writer of a football memoir, this confession is hard. It should be embarrassing but it isn't. The fact is that at school I was useless at sport, with the exception of sprinting. I could run fast. The school sorted out the tortoises from the hares by taking the whole of each year-group and have them run the length of a football pitch. I tended to win this, to my amazement. One day, in the street by our house, I happened to be with the Head Boy, who excelled at every sport from marathon to egg and spoon, and although I didn't usually play with him because I was of a lower order, we ran, with another boy, about 200 yards. I was beaten by only a few inches. In racing terms it was almost a dead heat. I remember his look at me. It was the kind of look you might give a donkey that went close in the Grand National.

But apart from that aberration, I was useless. I could never learn to swim; I hated the gym; I never had the proper kit for anything and so I was one of the cowering, pathetic group of non-starters who loitered in the changing room until ordered out wearing just underpants and socks, the target of all the bullies and comedians of the school.

On most occasions the pathetic failures managed to avoid games. This was because the Head was becoming worried about the casualties: in one year, there were three cases of fractured bones on the rugby pitch, two broken arms in weight-lifting; concussion in the yard and three collapses in the cross-country. After all, the sports in the school were organised by a man with the determination of Captain Scott and the brutality of Himmler. That was a recipe for suffering of a very high order.

One games teacher specialised in creating humiliation, indignity and disgrace. His method was to set unrealistic tasks and not prepare you for them. A boy might try the wall bars up to the high ceiling, then get stuck between rungs. The teacher would allow the ridicule to have its way before doing anything. Then there were the ropes – we non-sport lads could not grasp the method of climbing a rope by wrapping the thing around the leg and then gradually scaling the heights. The result was that the sports lads had done the ropes and moved on, while three inept hopeless cases swung at the bottom of the rope, hands red as fresh blood and shamed cheeks to match.

Yet failure gave me the freedom to be the horrible little swot I was deep down in the soul. At 12, I was finally beginning to read without having my stubby fat finger under every word and my tongue weirdly sticking out of my mouth. I was also completely hooked on foreign words as well, and loved French. My nickname changed from Paddy to Monsieur. 'Paddy' had been given me because I did accents and impressions and my Irish accent was so bad that the lads teased me mercilessly. But 'Monsieur' began to be my name outside and inside: I was what would now be called a geek. While most other boys were playing rugger or trying archery (three more casualties in the first month of this new sport) I was in the Stamp Club.

I was a stamp-collector because of the foreign words on the stamps. I learned all the words for countries in their own language, such as Suomi for Finland and Osterreich for Austria. In the 1960s, popular culture began to be flooded with gimmicky things for kids and I loved the wordy ones. There was a series of chewing-gum cards with information on each country of the world, along with six words in the language. This was paradise, second only to collecting Wills cards of stars and jockeys, and PG Tips cards with animals and birds. Each card would have facts about population and industry, and then there would be the foreign words. I was so obsessed with collecting language, wherever it appeared strange and interesting, that if the word had existed to describe my 'condition', I would have been treated for some kind of fashionable disorder.

The truth is that failure became fun. To fail to meet the standards of the school ethos meant that you were crap at technical drawing and you would never make an apprentice in engineering. That suited me just fine. I was happy to make up sentences in French and read *King Solomon's Mines*. The one activity I did enjoy in that technical production-line for future fitters, turners and draughtsmen was using the forge. I contrived to stretch the manufacture of a toasting-fork last for a whole term just because I enjoyed belting metal on the anvil. Mr Kirby must have suspected me of malingering – a favourite word at the time – but he was far too busy with the successes than to bother about the failures.

Still, under all the word-fixation there was still the prevailing macho ideology of 'proving yourself' in some way. It was inevitable that I would go into football after leaving school, but in between the 8-0 thrashings and the physical deprivations of Sunday in the park there was poetry. In my case poetry has been a part of my life since 1969. That has nothing to do with the moon landing or with Viet Nam. It has to do with my love of imagining myself to be a displaced person, a 'superfluous man' as the Russians call it, an outsider lodging in the margins of Bohemia, rotting in a limbo writing self-indulgent lyrics and sonnets on spiritual barrenness and on heroes such as Milton and Baudelaire.

I began to be involved in poetry readings and that was another version of the beautiful joy of failure. There is a very entertaining book to be written on failed literary gigs; I could compile an encyclopaedia of literary disasters from the demi-monde of the poetry reading. I have read to three people for an hour in a village hall; I have read in cafés while families ate pizza and told jokes; I have read to other poets who applauded me, and then sat down to listen to and applaud them in turn. I once had a reading arranged with another poet and we had no-one there except three kid hammering a ball against the wall outside. We went to the pub.

I have even mixed football with poetry readings, and I recall one event when I read a poem about goalies to a solemn, intellectually focused audience and they wrinkled their brows, unable to grasp the textual references – to such luminaries of the keeper's art as 'Piggy' Lawrence of Liverpool and Joe Corrigan of Manchester City. However, when the topic of football and failure is raised, a Leeds fan has to grudgingly speak the name of Gary Sprake. He was not a failure: in fact he was magnificent, and a joy to watch, but he suffered from the evil of the football fan's propensity to snigger at one mistake and forget all the skill.

Gary suffered from this because what circulates about him in footy talk is largely the disgusting emphasis on 'Careless Hands' – stemming from the infamous game at Anfield in 1967 when he had the ball in his grasp and was preparing to chuck the ball out to Terry Cooper when he saw Callaghan, a Liverpool player, too close for the throw to be made. In that second of indecision, the ball sprang from his hand and trickled into his net. The sick and twisted Liverpool tannoy man played the song *Careless Hands* at half-time. My short poem, recited at readings, set out to put the record straight:

> Never blame Gary, caught in two minds by the net;
> It's the tannoy man who should carry the can.
> I hope that Scouser's pee'd his best trousers
> And his crotch is eternally wet.

When I began, around 1975, a poetry reading was usually an uneasy, nervous occasion at which the poet, broody and angry, sat at a table waiting to be introduced by a posh and cultured MC. Then the poet would stand, smile like a man about to be hanged, and shuffle hundreds of sheets of paper, apologising for being in a mess and not having prepared for the event. Then the audience of three would be restless. A string of nervous readings would follow, with the same words spoken in between each poem: 'The next poem is about...'

Some of the most disastrous but successful readings were those in which one poet read to just one other person or the poet arrived at the venue to find the caretaker waiting to open up, but then nobody came so it was called off and the door was never opened.

The most challenging reading was at a rugby club. I was in a room next door to a bar full of one-armed bandits and heavy, loud prop-forwards who were telling jokes as if they wanted to be heard in Germany. I ploughed on manfully, shouting the poems, and the audience gradually dwindled as they thought there was going to be a fight. The MC was ready to go in next door and yell at the oafs who had no sensitivity to poetry etc....

But failure is also in the world of the supporter today. I still teach adults but I now indulge in the celebration of footy failure and mediocrity by driving 120 miles on Saturdays to support a team who exemplify all the most alluring qualities of joyful failure. Every year they fight hard to stay in the same division of the football league; every year they begin with promise and confidence, new faces in the squad and usually a new 'suit' in the boardroom, and every year they entertain with ever-new versions of mediocrity. I am beyond the stage of even breaking into a run, although I reckon I could still pass a ball well or head a solid clearance – as long as nobody watching expected to see success.

My son has the same relish for footy mediocrity I have always had, and he teaches English like his dad, following in the noble tradition of disseminating the love of great writing, creativity and the skill of not being too bothered if everything read is not Shakespeare. Football is never in danger of replacing religion with us; it stays firmly in the category of art for art's sake. In other words, if a game has a few splendidly ambitious long passes and a terrific point-blank stop by the keeper, then a 5-0 defeat matters not. Football – playing or supporting – is about enjoying the clownish failure of being a man. We learn slowly, with partners and careers as much as with sport, and the failures are more entertaining than the small successes.

The future is bright. The team (name not given to avoid controversy) will almost certainly finish tenth in the league at the end of next year, but that will be a joyful, satisfied tenth, earned by effort and willpower, missing the dizzy heights of success by maybe just a few points. The joys of being nearly there are hard to explain. It's partly a fear of success and partly the need to struggle for everything. But try telling the old lie to the die-hard supporters that 'Playing is more important than winning' and you will see the limits of that line of thought.

Mediocrity has its virtues. Best to be a middling sort of bloke. I've watched hundreds of new faces turn out for various teams, just to sink into oblivion in no time. Why? Because they were bruited to the terraces as being the next Bobby Charlton. No, broadcast the guy as a mediocrity and all will be well. On the first match of the season, when optimism can peep out for once, out from under the dark blanket of despair that footy fans wrap around themselves, the new players should be announced thus:

> *And at left back let's welcome Harry Hogbottom, local lad, come up through the local leagues, likes a pint and a pastie... a man with mediocre talents but who will die for the club. He scored one goal for Scrotum Athletic and that was a fluke, but now he's overcome his groin problems and will put some fairly true grit into our defence... (applause)*

As for my steel town: Scunthorpe prospers in spite of the setbacks. The 'Iron' are now in League One after relegation from the Championship (2011 season). Faces watch the newspaper billboards anxiously as different organisations buy the steelworks, and there is news of lay-offs and slackening in production. But this is a good, steady, workful town; its people make you proud in their graft and family values. I may be a Tyke by birth, and this memoir has been largely about growing up a Yorkie, but in this town, a place between worlds – not Yorkshire and not Lincolnshire but 'North Lincolnshire' and formerly 'Humberside' there is everyday evidence of caring and sharing and people still wish you good morning.

Football has given the town a rise, a spring in the step, as Don Revie did for Leeds back in the 1960s. As I write this in 2011, the Iron are the only league team left fighting in Lincolnshire. A friend suggested that they should be renamed Lincolnshire United because the others – Grimsby, Lincoln, Boston and Gainsborough – have all dropped from the proper leagues into oblivion.

As for me, I'm still drunk on words and taking every opportunity to infect other people with that wonderful obsession. Like the player in me, I don't like excuses. I would struggle to think of excuses for not writing, to match some of the richest excuses for not playing well – such as chapped legs, dazzling sun, carrying a knock, being flat-footed, having the effects of bad beer… but for the wordsmith life, there is no way out of the deadline, of completing the page or the chapter. Life does the same: it closes in and the end of the story has to be handled effectively. So it was with the end of my Mam. Dad had died many years ago – back in 1972. Mam had married again, but not been happy until her later years. When she went, it was the closing bars of a big but unsung song.

The Leeds story? Well, in one sense, it ended with my mother's death in March 2011. We have so many different narratives of ourselves and our native places, and one of the strongest of these is the sense that we are eventually left at the end of the line. For years there may be dozens of relatives: aunts, uncles, cousins, grandparents – and then they all fall away into the endless dark, and then so do the parents. My mother's death was such for me. My brother and I stood at Cottingley Hall cemetery, wedged between Elland Road on one side and Churwell on the other. The geography of its past was with me stronger than ever that chilly day in April as the man from the funeral directors asked us if we had a prayer to say. He stood there, the phial of ashes in his hands, and I said that I would like him to say something. He said some good words for that occasion and then sprinkled what was left of Mam in a cross-shape over the turf where the Wade ancestors lay.

As the eldest, I was left at the end of the line. Suddenly I had the feeling that I was the aged one, the next to go. What can you do but joke in the face of death? On the way to Mam's funeral, I said to my brother, 'Some people will do anything to go to Elland Road.' She would have smiled.

There we stood, not knowing what to say or do. My life in Leeds and my later life in Lincolnshire came to that: the memory of the early days in Churwell was as strong as ever;

I could see the whole village in my head. Up the hill, on the left was the cricket ground where dads and uncles had worn the whites and slogged for the boundary; to the right, across the Tanhouse, was the football pitch where Dad had played as a stopper. Further on was the Working Men's Club where tales of past games were recounted and retired heroes spun yarns over their pints of bitter. The Old Road – a Roman Road – led to the Tanhouse, and along there the landscape to one side was dominated by fields of rhubarb, where I learned about the follies of plucking green stalks to chew on, as this was always followed by belly-ache.

Surely we all have a place like that in our heads: put I guess that writers and poets crank it all up into a personal mythic tale. I'm not ashamed to say that I've maybe done that. But then the small people have huge stories. It's just that most publishers only want to know about celebrities – unlike most readers, I would guess. Some of my lot were celebrities in their neck of the Yorkshire woods. Grandma Wade, Nellie, was a midwife and layer-out in her village; Granddad Wade was a notorious character with charm by the cart-load; Uncle Alf made misery into a fine art. All this was known and celebrated. The Yorkshire face is generally grim but it lights up at three things: a free pint, a garden shed with a kettle, and a goal for the local team.

History, past time, years nibbled away by the hungry jaws of time. And we stood looking this way and that. Billy Bremner's statue not far off, and the pubs where Leeds players and supporters from Revie's time laughed and joked, relishing the sight of one of the best teams ever made in the English game. Surrounded by aged tombstones chipped at by centuries of Yorkshire weather, I saw in my mind the people from my bloodline: miners, seamen, coal merchants, traders, a midwife, seamstresses, shop-keeper, bookies, potter, carter and tanner. These were trades closely tied to Leeds history, people rooted in Hunslet and Holbeck, Beeston and Morley. With these in mind, here is a poem from my copious notebooks for my Dad and the rest who worshipped Leeds United and longed for Saturday afternoon. It's not at all about flowers or fantasies:

Keeper

Stretching his frame to fill the goal,
Running on the spot, spitting in the mud,
Doing everything he could to plug the hole
In that leaky defence. His yells, terrifying,
Weakened defenders' knees, seared his throat.
Solid as a plank of hard wood on that white line.
Most of all, his gloves, most manly and swanky.
And his only hidden nightmare, the penalty,
Him soaring into cool Sunday air, the ball not there
And the crowd of six saying, 'Other way, lanky...'

Then I thought of my new home and the steelmen, and I smiled at the old rivalry of the Iron, Scunthorpe United, and Leeds. There have been recent games in which the current Leeds team have been well beaten in Scunthorpe, notably a 5-1 drubbing in a fierce wind at the Old Showground. I wondered if Revie's face would have cracked at that. I think he did smile, but it was sometimes a bit like looking at a letter-box slit. I saw him once out of Elland Road. He was visiting Les Cocker in St James's Hospital. He smiled at the staff and seemed to be at ease. Maybe he'd already done the team-sheet and was happy to arrive with toffees and a few cheery stories. Revie looked like the Head Boy on best behaviour, polite and restrained, but with a tremor in him that suggested he might implode at any second. In this he was just like Arsene Wenger at Arsenal today: you're rooting for him because you know by his face that winning a match is better than a month in Paradise with free beer and Billy Connolly telling stories. You always felt that Revie's emotional life was not worn on his sleeve – it was dyed into the skin of his face, or maybe like a mask he slipped on before every game.

It was time to turn towards the year 2011 and negotiate the tangled arteries of Leeds roadways and the row and hum of modern Yorkshire, its thoroughfares as confused and mystified as its residents, and to turn towards Scunthorpe, its shops depleted and its history shovelled away, but its people hearty and resilient, still believing in families, children and the future with or without steel.

Football in Leeds once had a bad reputation. The fans were supposed to be the shame of the land. But this is down to the media in most cases; what Revie showed us was that having a kit like Real Madrid, pure white, might make you look like ten trainee doctors and a man in a green jersey shouting at the back, but somehow it helped in that priceless commodity of self-belief, and it started something magical, like Clough at Forest or Ferguson at the Red Enemy across the Pennines (I say that very grudgingly).

Like all memories, my thoughts began with a clear perception of how I thought it was back in c. 1950, and then the rose-coloured spectacles took over, as they always do. Life was tough, that was for sure. But again, when they played footy or cricket in Churwell, boy they did it with gusto. They ate their rabbit soup and their black pudding with the same zeal, and the concept of a supermarket was in the realms of science fiction. The old Churwellers – descended from the 'churls by the well' in Domesday Book times – lived by collecting fire-wood, selling carrots from the garden, swapping jumpers for trousers and then trousers for jumpers, and danced and sang in the spaces between hard labour.

Then they went down the road, past the prefabs, past the dyeworks, past the football pitch, to join the forebears.

At Cottingley, Did I hear the Revie roar, a swell of ghostly voices raised above the ground, as we drove towards town? You bet. Kicked into touch? Only until the next game.

Checklist

A-Z of the Park

Back Pass

One of the riskiest tests of skill for Sunday players. This is the pass back to the keeper by a player. The normal result of this is that the ball is placed at the feet of the opposing striker, who then scores. Or the pass may stick in the mud around the goalmouth, thus causing a HOSPITAL BALL for the keeper who rashly tries to retrieve the ball before the striker kicks it.

Banana Shot

A curving drive restricted to those players who have skill. This is why it is sometimes called a 'Brazilian.' Attempts to fire such a shot at goal on the Park result in either a member of the crowd (the man and dog) being injured or the shot goes high and loops over the stand.

Bench

In Sunday football, it's a bench, that's all. But if we're talking subs, then yes, there may be one. He's the chubby lad who wheezes on a fag and moans about not getting a game, or he's the one as thin as a streak of bacon who gives a hard stare at the man whose shirt he thinks he should be wearing.

Blouse, Big Girl's

A purely sexist term of abuse, applied to a perceptibly useless player – that is, useless in the sense that he does not risk a broken leg by committing '200 percent' when given a hospital ball.

Captain

He is the player with the loudest voice and the need to collect subs, so that he can buy the beer and look impressively in charge.

Clogger

An out-moded term for a guy with more enthusiasm than skill. Strangely, he gathers grudging respect – but only if his team wins.

Crowd

A man and a dog. But occasionally a wife or girlfriend will come, sometimes bringing a child and pointing out 'Daddy' on the field, and so a negative image of the hapless father is rooted in the child's mind forever.

Donkey

A term used of a player with no skill or finesse but who runs around chasing shadows and bumps into his own players, misses the crosses, passes to nobody and deceivingly, looks quite fit for purpose in the warm-up.

Early Bath

This refers to a man being sent off for bad conduct such as violent behaviour, swearing at the ref, doing a goal celebration by removing his pants and jock-strap etc. But in Sunday footy there are no baths, so it really means an early sulk.

First Aid

This is a bucket of water and a packet of Elastoplast. The better teams have a 'magic spray' as well, although this is considered to be a gay addition to the equipment. As noted earlier, a revolution is needed in this branch of Sunday football, with advanced medicine being applied, perhaps with an eye to the ageing players: kit should include a defibrillator, blood-pressure monitor and a shapely nurse, who must not be a wife or partner of a player.

Grudge

A petty hatred or resentment that festers in the player's soul until he can get his own back and kick the hell out of the guy who did his shin or elbowed him in the mush.

Handbags

This has become the generic term for any kind of petulant

disagreement, such as shoving, chest expanding, eye-to-eye stares and spitting, between two terriers on the pitch who refuse to back down and shake hands.

Hospital Ball

A pass made by an idiot which, if the player goes to try to collect, he will wake up in the Ward for Hopeless Cases at the local hospital. Often, a pass made by a team-mate who has a grudge.

Knock, carrying a..

This refers to a harsh clout on a limb and a sorry, undignified hobble until a manly piece of drama means that you will carry on – usually running off a knock.

Linesman

An official who is usually absent in Sunday park games. He is supposed to be the official who runs the line and helps to make off-side decisions and other observations on various offences. When such a person does actually appear, he usually has ironing-lines in his shorts and has a notebook tied to his wrist. Sometimes he has a tin hat and a bodyguard. Female lines people do not tend to get the abuse, but the rude words are still there, muttered with apologies, by the man and dog. When the lineslady does receive abuse, heads roll in the ranks of TV pundits.

Long Ball Game

The only way to play for most Sunday teams. You punt the ball upfield hopefully rather than with accuracy, and run the risk of abuse from crowd and team-mates as well. But it can work if your strikers are all grotesquely over six feet six inches tall with rubber necks.

Metatarsal Whatsit

The kind of injury you have if you want two weeks off so you can go to Madeira and play beach footy while sloshed.

Nutmeg

As in: 'He nutmegged the defender and slid the ball in.' This refers to a player putting the ball between the legs of an oncoming player. This makes the victim look so foolish that a foul inevitably follows, as the nutmegger is promptly clogged.

Off side

A football rule that is so elaborate that it can only be understood by women. But vaguely, in Sunday games, it can be used to shout abuse at any unpopular player. Tell someone he is offside and he checks position and makes a mistake. In fact, even football pundits have no idea about the offside rule but relish it as a discussion topic because it shows off laddish anorak knowledge to good effect.

Penalty

A put-up job making a goal easy. This tends to ruin a game and add needless drama, injecting so much stress into the players that grudges are born there. The best penalties are those in which the taker stubs his toe and misses the ball completely, and then feigns injury.

Played On

A player who is dreaming about the lunch-time pint after the game, or who is chatting up a passing young lady, will be caught in such a position that he is playing onside the opposing striker who is just about to burst the net with a pile-driver. Such a player usually buys the beer after the match.

Positions

The textbook is often ignored on this matter. A's position is vaguely defined as 'sweeper' or 'striker' but sometimes, as with the habits of little boys in the school playground, all ten outfield players may chase one pass. In most of my Sunday League days, someone had to shout abuse at me to stop me chasing every ball, just as I did when a nipper.

Pundit

A person, usually male, who has an opinion on all aspects of the game, has a few impressive statistics to hand, and bewails the death of the 'proper game' He can and does exist in the world of Sunday football, but is generally shunned except by other pundits, and they tend to vie for most macho opinions and most convincing production of facts from long-forgotten division four (old style) games. The pundit tends to know as much about Accrington Stanley as Chelsea, and can even tell you who Stanley actually was.

Referee

A pathetically sad man, often rotund and bald, who absorbs abuse for 90 minutes on the pitch. One story of a referee on the park in a Sunday league involves the local Mafia, a rabid dog and a death threat. The Mafia team won the day. The man who chooses to be a ref is often a guy who was always abused when a player and now gets revenge. The best ones make the ticking-off after a foul into grand opera. One ref in our league was so small that he only ever had a proper view of knees, so if he didn't have tall linesmen, you could cheat in a hundred different ways.

Ringer

In brief, the player brought in from some higher more esteemed team or background to do his bit for the mediocre lot – usually in a cup-tie or a relegation battle. Also:

The old crock who played for such and such united ten years ago but still can beat three men and score – or, the spritely young lad who prances about like Ronaldo and looks uncannily like the young lad who also plays for the top of the league but who now sports a beard.

Square Ball

Not a square ball – a pass across the pitch. These passes usually end up in the next field, the ball being chased by a dog, who stops play and then the player who kicked it gets some abuse.

Strip

A set of rank clothes in a large bag, dragged into the changing-room every Sunday, caked with dried mud, blood and spittle. The last player to arrive has to wear the smallest, most offensive shirt and socks, and his smell is then his best mode of attack on the opposition. If a wife or partner has washed the strip on perhaps one or two Sundays in the season, then the husband or male partner in question has to run the gauntlet of being accused of having gay leanings, and a less than acceptable interest in fashion.

Sweeper

Nothing to do with a brush or besom, although a brush would maybe be more effective – at least it could be used to trip a nippy winger.

The last line of defence, the man who props up the defence and covers for the centre-half. He is usually to be found up the pitch, fighting for breath after going up for a corner, striving with all his might to run back into position.

Tactics

'Get out there and kick arse.' Or, when there really is an important game coming up, tactics means very long and confused talk in the bar, concerning the danger-men in the enemy team (sorry, opposition). Every player has a tactical idea, and none are ever listened to, but his words are greeted with a laugh and 'Who do you think you are – Mourinho?' This then leads to a long discussion on the Portuguese 'Special One' and whether or not he is a tactical genius or just a man who looks sexy in a long coat, according to the missis.

Touchline

A white line marking the edge of the pitch which tends to be flexible, according to the linesman.

Trainer

A mysterious person who appears on the scene only when the Sunday team has reached a final and then the result actually matters.

Warm-Up

The exercise just before the game starts, in which various players pull ham-strings or have migraines. There have even been cases of players picking up a bug while in a warm-up, therefore defying medical science.

Zone

In professional football, a tactic involving each player having a defined area of the pitch in which to play. When applied in Sunday on the Park games, this results in players crashing into each other and then falling out about who was in and who was out of his zone.